Prairie Patchwork

Treasured Quilts and Tales of Time

Martha Walker

Martingale®
Create with Confidence

Martingale®
19021 120th Ave. NE, Ste. 102
Bothell, WA 98011-9511 USA
ShopMartingale.com

Printed in Hong Kong
25 24 23 22 21 20   8 7 6 5 4 3 2 1

Library of Congress Cataloging-in-Publication Data is available upon request.

ISBN: 978-1-68356-106-4

MISSION STATEMENT

We empower makers who use fabric and yarn to make life more enjoyable.

CREDITS

PUBLISHER AND CHIEF VISIONARY OFFICER
Jennifer Erbe Keltner

CONTENT DIRECTOR
Karen Costello Soltys

DESIGN MANAGER
Adrienne Smitke

MANAGING EDITOR
Tina Cook

PRODUCTION MANAGER
Regina Girard

ACQUISITIONS AND DEVELOPMENT EDITOR
Laurie Baker

COVER AND BOOK DESIGNER
Kathy Kotomaimoce

TECHNICAL EDITOR
Nancy Mahoney

PHOTOGRAPHERS
Adam Albright
Brent Kane

COPY EDITOR
Melissa Bryan

ILLUSTRATOR
Sandy Loi

SPECIAL THANKS
Photography for this book was taken at the homes of:
Lianne Anderson in Arlington, Washington
Karen Burns in Carnation, Washington
Tracie Fish in Kenmore, Washington
Julie Smiley in Des Moines, Iowa

Contents

Bonus project! Find Songbird Needlecase online at ShopMartingale.com/PrairiePatchwork.

Introduction

What would it have been like to be a Civil War widow in 1871, relocating more than 1,100 miles from home with three young children and making that journey in a covered wagon? How would the trek have been remembered by those children years later?

The quilts and projects I designed for this book illustrate the recollections of a young girl who makes an overland journey with her family from what is now West Virginia to Kansas in 1871, six years after the end of the War Between the States. Carrie's story is based upon my family records, beginning with the factual account of my great-great-grandfather David's death toward the end of the Civil War and the subsequent journey west embarked upon by my great-great-grandmother, Mahala, and her three children.

I can only speculate about what precipitated Mahala's decision to migrate to Kansas. Perhaps the war years were particularly difficult, given David and Mahala's proximity to some of the earliest conflicts of that war. They lived in the western part of Virginia, eerily near where the first land battles of the Civil War took place in the Tygart Valley region in 1861. The battles and skirmishes between Confederate troops and Union forces were concentrated in that small area of western Virginia and lasted the better part of 1861. The Battle of Corrick's Ford that summer took place just 30 miles south of David and Mahala's home. Farms and homesteads in the valley—willingly or unwillingly on the part of the families who lived there—became battlefields, housing camps, and fortifications. Soldiers dug pits, felled trees, constructed abatis, and moved in their artillery.

After the war's end, many more challenges surely faced Mahala, now a young widow with three children to rear alone. Like many others before her, perhaps she felt the West beckoning with the hope of a better life. Whatever the reason, she did, in fact, make the decision to migrate westward and settle in Kansas. At the time of their journey, Mahala's daughters were 15 and 9, and her youngest child, my great-grandfather, was 6 years old.

The following narrative describes the overland journey from western Virginia to Kansas from the perspective of the eldest daughter, Rebecca, whom I have renamed Carrie. Both fact and fiction are woven together to create Carrie's memoir. I tried to imagine, using firsthand accounts and research of the period, what a pioneer's journey might have been like from a young person's viewpoint. Carrie begins her account with the death of her father and preparations for the family's journey west. You'll find that each project represents a snapshot of her travels and her life after settlement, beginning with the quilt Hill Country on page 7 (leaving Virginia) and progressing to prairie-inspired projects representing her new home in Kansas, such as Prairie Spring (page 31) and Sunflower Fields (page 47). I hope you'll enjoy the journey!

~Martha

Carrie's Story

Many children were left fatherless after the War Between the States, and my sister, brother, and I were no exception.

Father was a corporal in the 6th Regiment of the West Virginia Volunteers. He was tasked with guarding the trains at the large depot at Grafton. He and Uncle Leander were both discharged in October of 1864, and they took a train to Wheeling to pick up their final pay. At Glovers Gap, their train collided head-on with another train. Father's chest and shoulder were crushed, and a large stove crushed Uncle Leander's leg. He was able to cut his leg free with a pocket knife, and now walks with a wooden leg. They were eventually found and taken back to Grafton and to a hospital.

Mother was notified of Father's injuries, and she left us in our grandparents' care so that she could go to Grafton to nurse him. Chills and fever came on the twelfth day, and Father died a week later. He was buried in the army cemetery there, and Mother came home to tell us the sorry news.

I was eight years old at the time, and the eldest of my siblings. Mother became quite dependent on me to help with the little ones—Eliza, who was three when father died, and Edward, who was just a baby.

A few years after the war's end, we began hearing excited talk of "free land" to the west, and later started noticing some of our neighbors leaving their homes in large wagons. The talk came closer to home when Mother's sister, Dorothy, and her husband, Uncle Leander, made the decision to travel to the new state of Kansas, where there

were large tracts of land still available to homesteaders. They were anxious to have us join them. Mother reluctantly agreed to make the move with them, but only after she was able to get her pension as a war widow approved.

Plans began to take shape, and I spent the next few years helping Mother make preparations for the journey—sewing two-bushel sacks to hold flour and cornmeal, smaller sacks for dried fruit, beans, rice, sugar, and coffee; feather ticks; a large cover for a wagon; and plain, serviceable clothing for us all. We made a large quantity of dip candles that would hopefully last us a full year. It was hard for me to conceive of what the long journey and new life would be like.

The year was 1871 when we finally said our tearful goodbyes to our loved ones, whom we suspected we would never see again. With two wagons loaded full, we were off to the West with Uncle Leander and Aunt Dorothy to claim a new home in Kansas.

~ Carrie, 1880

Hill Country

Our wagons loaded, Mother, my sister, my brother, and I said goodbye to Grandma and Grandpa and headed north toward Wheeling, where we would meet the Cumberland Road. We passed through the hills and down through the swamps, where the swamp milkweed, rosebuds, and Scarlet Beebalm painted the land with a riot of red, pink, and purple.

FINISHED QUILT: 39" × 53⅛"

Materials

Yardage is based on 42"-wide fabric.

1⅜ yards *total* of assorted pink and beige prints for pieced columns

1½ yards of cream print for pieced columns, sashing, and border

⅓ yard of pink print for binding

2½ yards of fabric for backing

45" × 60" piece of batting

Cutting

Cut all pieces across the width of the fabric unless otherwise noted. All measurements include ¼" seam allowances.

From the assorted pink and beige prints, cut a *total* of:

88 rectangles, 2" × 8"

2 squares, 3⅜" × 3⅜"; cut the squares into quarters diagonally to yield 8 triangles

From the *lengthwise grain* of the cream print, cut:

2 strips, 4½" × 39"

3 strips, 3½" × 45⅛"

2 strips, 2½" × 45⅛"

From the remainder of the cream print, cut:

42 squares, 3⅜" × 3⅜"; cut the squares into quarters diagonally to yield 168 triangles

From the pink print for binding, cut:

5 strips, 2" × 42"

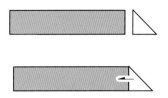

WESTWARD HO

Swamp milkweed, also known as pink milkweed, is a member of the milkweed family. It loves moisture and seeks the sunny areas along swamps, marshes, and stream banks. Native to most of North America, the plant blooms in the summer months with showy clusters of pink and light purple flowers that have a subtle, sweet vanilla scent.

Butterflies such as swallowtails and fritillaries are attracted to the blooms, and the monarch butterfly is particularly drawn to this plant—the "king of the butterflies" will lay its eggs only *on milkweed.*

Making the Pieced Columns

Press seam allowances in the directions indicated by the arrows.

1. Select one pink or beige rectangle and two cream triangles. Sew the triangles by their short edges to opposite ends of the rectangle, noting the orientation of the triangles. Make 72 units.

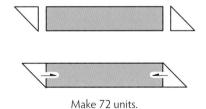

Make 72 units.

2. In the same manner, sew a cream triangle to just one end of 16 pink or beige rectangles.

Make 16 units.

3. Join a pink or beige triangle and a cream triangle along their short edges. Make eight triangle units.

Make 8 units.

4. Lay out 18 units from step 1, four units from step 2, and two triangle units from step 3 in a column as shown. Join the units, adding the triangle units last. Use a ruler and rotary cutter to trim the top and bottom of the column even with the triangle units. Make four columns measuring 6⅞" × 45⅛", including seam allowances.

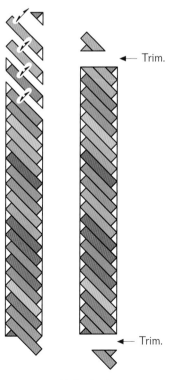

← Trim.

← Trim.

Make 4 columns, 6⅞" × 45⅛".

Assembling the Quilt Top

1. Lay out the columns and cream 3½" × 45⅛" strips as shown in the quilt assembly diagram below. Join the columns to make the quilt-top center, which should measure 35" × 45⅛", including seam allowances.

2. Sew the cream 2½" × 45⅛" strips to opposite sides of the quilt top. Sew the cream 4½" × 39" strips to the top and bottom edges. The completed quilt top should measure 39" × 53⅛".

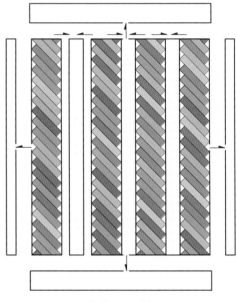

Quilt assembly

Finishing the Quilt

For detailed instructions about any of the finishing steps, go to ShopMartingale.com/HowtoQuilt for free, downloadable information.

1. Layer the backing, batting, and quilt top. Baste the layers together.

2. Quilt by hand or machine. The quilt shown is machine quilted with a feather motif in the pieced columns and the top and bottom borders. Straight vertical lines and a chain of connected circles are quilted in the cream columns and side borders.

3. Use the pink 2"-wide strips to make binding, and then attach the binding to the quilt.

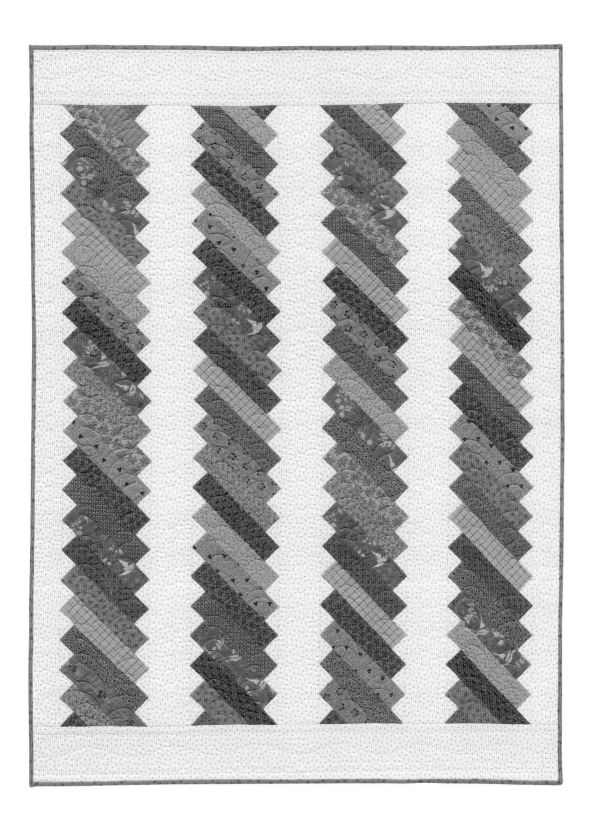

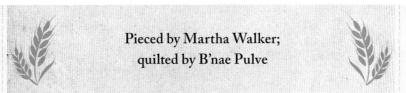

Pieced by Martha Walker;
quilted by B'nae Pulve

Cumberland Road

Wheeling was bustling with activity, and we were not alone on our journey west. Cumberland Road was crowded with what looked like hundreds of wagons of all sizes, accompanied by horses, mules, cattle, and oxen. I was in awe of the huge suspension bridge that we used to cross over the Ohio River. For miles and miles we traveled, sometimes stopping at small farms along the way to purchase fresh eggs or other foodstuffs. On clear nights the sky seemed larger than it ever had at home, and I felt very small, indeed.

FINISHED QUILT: 71½" × 83½"
FINISHED BLOCKS: 11" × 11"

Materials

Yardage is based on 42" wide fabric.

2⅞ yards of cream solid for blocks

3¼ yards of black print for blocks, sashing, inner border, and binding

3½ yards of red print for blocks and outer border

7⅞ yards *total* of assorted tan, red, and black prints (referred to collectively as "dark") for blocks and sashing

5¼ yards of fabric for backing

80" × 92" rectangle of batting

Cutting

Cut all pieces across the width of the fabric unless otherwise noted. All measurements include ¼" seam allowances.

From the cream solid, cut:

2 strips, 3¾" × 42"; crosscut into 15 squares, 3¾" × 3¾"

3 strips, 1¾" × 42"; crosscut into 60 squares, 1¾" × 1¾"

37 strips, 1½" × 42"; crosscut into:
    37 strips, 1½" × 24"
    30 rectangles, 1½" × 5½"

4 strips, 3½" × 24"

2 strips, 5½" × 24"

From the *crosswise grain* of the black print, cut:

4 strips, 2⅛" × 42"; crosscut into 60 squares, 2⅛" × 2⅛"

16 strips, 1½" × 24"

From the *lengthwise grain* of the black print, cut:

2 strips, 2½" × 71½"

2 strips, 2½" × 63½"

5 strips, 2" × 65"

Continued on page 14

Continued from page 13

From the *crosswise grain* of the red print, cut:

20 strips, 1½" × 24"

From the *lengthwise grain* of the red print, cut:

2 strips, 4½" × 75½"

2 strips, 4½" × 71½"

15 squares, 3" × 3"

From the assorted dark prints, cut a *total* of:

156 strips, 1½" × 24"

20 squares, 1½" × 1½"

Making the Star and Chain Blocks

Press seam allowances open unless the direction of the arrows in the diagrams indicates otherwise.

1. Draw a diagonal line from corner to corner on the wrong side of each black 2⅛" square. Align two squares on opposite corners of a cream 3¾" square, right sides together. The marked squares should overlap in the center. Sew ¼" from both sides of the drawn lines. Cut on the drawn lines to make two units.

2. Place a marked square on the cream corner of a unit from step 1, right sides together and noting the direction of the marked line. Sew ¼" from both sides of the drawn line. Cut the unit apart on the drawn line. Repeat with the remaining marked square and unit from step 1 to yield four flying-geese units. Make a total of 60 flying-geese units measuring 1¾" × 3", including seam allowances.

Make 60 units, 1¾" × 3".

3. Lay out four flying-geese units, four cream 1¾" squares, and one red 3" square in three rows of three. Sew the pieces into rows. Join the rows to make a star unit. Make 15 units measuring 5½" square, including seam allowances.

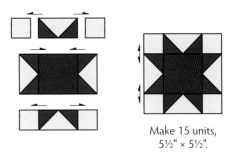

Make 15 units, 5½" × 5½".

4. Join three cream 1½" × 24" strips and two red 1½" × 24" strips along their long edges to make strip set A. Make two strip sets measuring 5½" × 24", including seam allowances. Crosscut the strip sets into 30 A segments, 1½" × 5½".

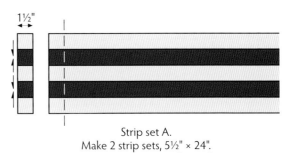

Strip set A.
Make 2 strip sets, 5½" × 24".
Cut 30 segments, 1½" × 5½".

5. Sew red 1½" × 24" strips to opposite sides of a cream 3½" × 24" strip to make strip set B. Make two strip sets measuring 5½" × 24", including seam allowances. Crosscut the strip sets into 30 B segments, 1½" × 5½".

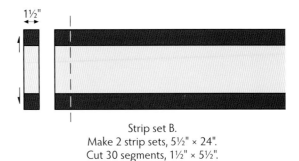

Strip set B.
Make 2 strip sets, 5½" × 24".
Cut 30 segments, 1½" × 5½".

6. Using 1½" × 24" strips, join two black strips, four dark strips, three cream strips, and two red strips in the order shown to make strip set C. Make two strip sets measuring 11½" × 24", including seam allowances. Crosscut the strip sets into 30 C segments, 1½" × 11½".

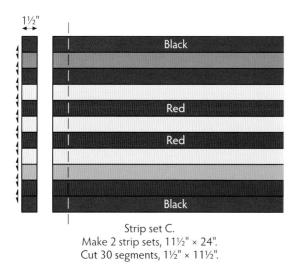

Strip set C.
Make 2 strip sets, 11½" × 24".
Cut 30 segments, 1½" × 11½".

7. Join four dark 1½" × 24" strips, two cream 1½" × 24" strips, two red 1½" × 24" strips, and one cream 3½" × 24" strip in the order shown to make strip set D. Make two strip sets measuring 11½" × 24", including seam allowances. Crosscut the strip sets into 30 D segments, 1½" × 11½".

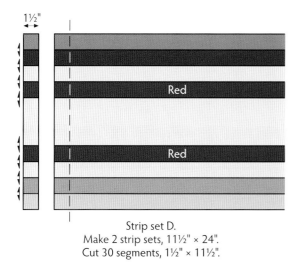

Strip set D.
Make 2 strip sets, 11½" × 24".
Cut 30 segments, 1½" × 11½".

8. Join two dark 1½" × 24" strips, two cream 1½" × 24" strips, two red 1½" × 24" strips, and one cream 5½" × 24" strip in the order shown to make strip set E. Make two strip sets measuring 11½" × 24", including seam allowances. Crosscut the strip sets into 30 E segments, 1½" × 11½".

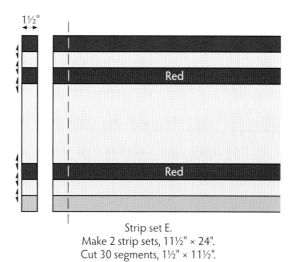

Strip set E.
Make 2 strip sets, 11½" × 24".
Cut 30 segments, 1½" × 11½".

9. Join one star unit, two A segments, two B segments, and two cream 1½" × 5½" rectangles to make a center row. Make 15 rows measuring 5½" × 11½", including seam allowances.

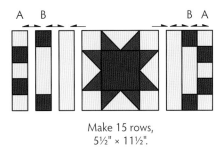

Make 15 rows,
5½" × 11½".

10. Lay out two C segments, two D segments, two E segments, and one center row from step 9 as shown. Join the segments and rows to make a Star and Chain block. Make 15 blocks measuring 11½" square, including seam allowances.

Make 15 blocks,
11½" × 11½".

Making the Postage Stamp Blocks

1. Using 1½" × 24" strips, join eight dark strips, two black strips, and one cream strip in the order shown to make strip set F. Make two

strip sets measuring 11½" × 24", including seam allowances. Crosscut the strip sets into 30 F segments, 1½" × 11½".

1½"

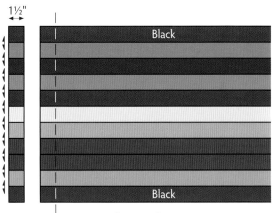

Strip set F.
Make 2 strip sets, 11½" × 24".
Cut 30 segments, 1½" × 11½".

WESTWARD HO

The Cumberland Road (also known as the National Road) was the first major highway built by the US government. Construction began in 1811 and continued into the late 1830s, creating more than 600 miles of roadway. The road connected the Potomac and Ohio Rivers and provided a main pathway west for thousands of settlers from states such as Maryland, Pennsylvania, Virginia, and Ohio. The Cumberland Road originally ended in Vandalia, Illinois, but was later extended into Missouri.

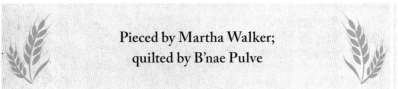

Pieced by Martha Walker;
quilted by B'nae Pulve

3. Using 1½" × 24" strips, join eight dark strips, two cream strips, and one black strip in the order shown to make strip set H. Make six strip sets measuring 11½" × 24", including seam allowances. Crosscut the strip sets into 79 H segments, 1½" × 11½". Set aside 49 segments to use when assembling the quilt top.

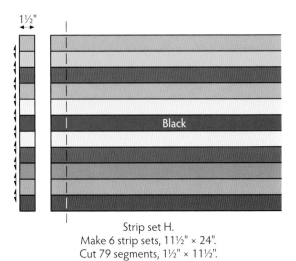

Strip set H.
Make 6 strip sets, 11½" × 24".
Cut 79 segments, 1½" × 11½".

2. Join 11 dark strips to make strip set G. Make six strip sets measuring 11½" × 24", including seam allowances. Crosscut the strip sets into 90 G segments, 1½" × 11½".

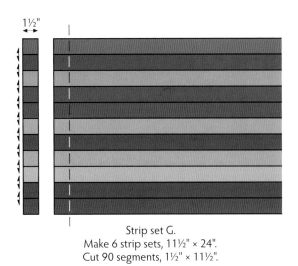

Strip set G.
Make 6 strip sets, 11½" × 24".
Cut 90 segments, 1½" × 11½".

4. Using 1½" × 24" strips, join three cream strips, six dark strips, and two black strips in the order shown to make strip set I, which should measure 11½" × 24", including seam allowances. Crosscut the strip set into 15 I segments, 1½" × 11½".

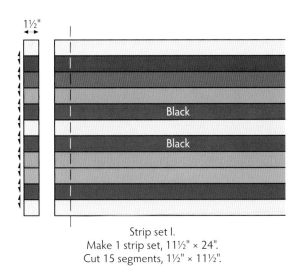

Strip set I.
Make 1 strip set, 11½" × 24".
Cut 15 segments, 1½" × 11½".

5. Lay out two F segments, six G segments, two H segments, and one I segment in the order shown. Join the segments to make a Postage Stamp block. Make 15 blocks measuring 11½" square, including seam allowances.

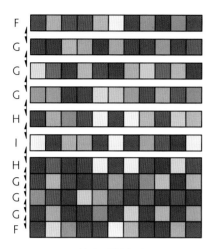

Make 15 blocks,
11½" × 11½".

Assembling the Quilt Top

1. Join three Postage Stamp blocks, two Star-and-Chain blocks, and four H segments to make row 1. Make three rows measuring 11½" × 59½", including seam allowances.

Block row 1.
Make 3 rows, 11½" × 59½".

2. Join three Star-and-Chain blocks, two Postage Stamp blocks, and four H segments to make row 2. Make three rows measuring 11½" × 59½", including seam allowances.

Block row 2.
Make 3 rows, 11½" × 59½".

3. Join five H segments and four dark 1½" squares to make a sashing row. Make five rows measuring 1½" × 59½", including seam allowances.

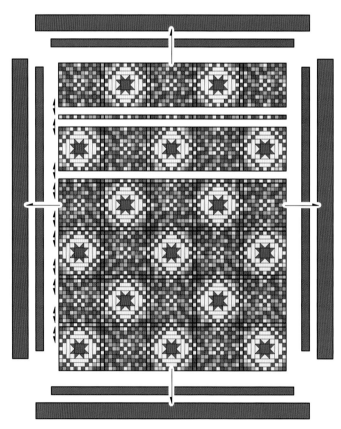

Sashing row.
Make 5 rows, 1½" × 59½".

4. Lay out block rows 1 and 2 as shown in the quilt assembly diagram below. Place the sashing rows between the block rows. Join the rows to make the quilt-top center, which should measure 59½" × 71½", including seam allowances.

5. Sew the black 2½" × 71½" strips to opposite sides of the quilt center. Sew the black 2½" × 63½" strips to the top and bottom edges. The quilt top should measure 63½" × 75½", including seam allowances.

6. Sew the red 4½" × 75½" strips to opposite sides of the quilt top. Sew the red 4½" × 71½" strips to the top and bottom edges. The completed quilt top should measure 71½" × 83½".

Finishing the Quilt

For detailed instructions about any of the finishing steps, go to ShopMartingale.com/HowtoQuilt for free, downloadable information.

1. Layer the backing, batting, and quilt top. Baste the layers together.

2. Quilt by hand or machine. The quilt shown is machine quilted with straight lines stitched diagonally in both directions through the squares. Feathers, circles, and curved lines are stitched around the star and curved lines are quilted in the center of the star. The inner border features circles and the outer border is quilted with feathers.

3. Use the black 2"-wide strips to make binding, and then attach the binding to the quilt.

Quilt assembly

St. Clair Sawmill

We left the Cumberland Road at Jefferson City, Missouri, and found our way to Harrisonville, Missouri, where we would spend the winter with friends. There we made arrangements with a local sawmill on the Osage River to have lumber shipped to Kansas at some future time, after we claimed our quarter section of land.

FINISHED QUILT: 69½" × 81½"
FINISHED BLOCK: 7½" × 7½"

Materials

Yardage is based on 42"-wide fabric. Fat quarters are 18"× 21".

3⅛ yards *total* of assorted beige prints for Sawmill blocks, Sawmill triangles, and sashing

1⅝ yards *total* of assorted medium and dark brown, gold, rust, and red prints (referred to collectively as "dark") for Sawmill blocks and triangles

⅓ yard of beige print A for Friendship Star blocks and side triangles

⅓ yard of brown print A for Friendship Star blocks and side triangles

½ yard *total* of 2 different rust prints for Friendship Star blocks and side triangles

1 fat quarter of red print for Friendship Star blocks

1⅛ yards of cream solid for sashing and outer border

1⅛ yards of brown print B for sashing and outer border

⅜ yard of rust plaid for inner border

⅜ yard of beige print B for middle border

⅜ yard of beige print C for middle border

1⅜ yards of rust print for outer border and binding

5 yards of fabric for backing

78" × 90" piece of batting

Cutting

Cut all pieces across the width of the fabric unless otherwise noted. All measurements include ¼" seam allowances.

SAWMILL BLOCKS

From the assorted beige prints, cut a *total* of:

18 sets of 2 matching squares, 2¾" × 2¾"

18 sets of 8 matching squares, 2⅜" × 2⅜"

From the assorted dark prints, cut a *total* of:

18 sets of 2 matching squares, 2¾" × 2¾"

18 sets of 8 matching squares, 2⅜" × 2⅜"

Continued on page 23

Continued from page 21

SAWMILL SIDE AND CORNER TRIANGLES

From the assorted beige prints, cut a *total* of:

6 squares, 4½" × 4½"; cut the squares into quarters diagonally to yield 24 large triangles

10 sets of 4 matching squares, 2⅜" × 2⅜"

4 sets of 2 matching squares, 2⅜" × 2⅜"

7 squares, 2⅜" × 2⅜"; cut the squares in half diagonally to yield 14 small triangles

From the assorted dark prints, cut a *total* of:

1 square, 4½" × 4½"; cut the square into quarters diagonally to yield 4 large triangles

10 squares, 2¾" × 2¾"

10 sets of 4 matching squares, 2⅜" × 2⅜"

4 sets of 2 matching squares, 2⅜" × 2⅜"

7 squares, 2⅜" × 2⅜"; cut the squares in half diagonally to yield 14 small triangles

FRIENDSHIP STAR BLOCKS AND SIDE TRIANGLES

From beige print A, cut:

4 strips, 2⅜" × 42"; crosscut into 56 squares, 2⅜" × 2⅜"

From brown print A, cut:

4 strips, 2⅜" × 42"; crosscut into 56 squares, 2⅜" × 2⅜"

From the 2 different rust prints, cut a *total* of:

21 sets of 4 matching squares, 2" × 2"

7 sets of 2 matching squares, 2" × 2"

14 squares, 2⅜" × 2⅜"; cut the squares in half diagonally to yield 28 triangles

From the red print, cut:

3 strips, 2" × 21"; crosscut into 21 squares, 2" × 2"

7 squares, 2⅜" × 2⅜"; cut the squares in half diagonally to yield 14 triangles

SASHING, BORDERS, AND BINDING

From the cream solid, cut:

7 strips, 4¾" × 42"; crosscut into 52 squares, 4¾" × 4¾"

From brown print B, cut:

7 strips, 4¾" × 42"; crosscut into 52 squares, 4¾" × 4¾"

From the assorted beige prints, cut a *total* of:

96 rectangles, 2" × 8"

From the rust print, cut:

22 strips, 2" × 42"

From the rust plaid, cut:

4 strips, 2¾" × 42"

From beige print B, cut:

4 strips, 2¾" × 42"

From beige print C, cut:

4 strips, 2½" × 42"

Making the Sawmill Blocks

For each block, you'll need two matching beige 2¾" squares, two matching dark 2¾" squares, eight matching 2⅜" squares from a different beige print, and eight matching dark 2⅜" squares. Instructions are for making one block. Press seam allowances in the directions indicated by the arrows.

1. Lay out two beige 2¾" squares and two dark 2¾" squares in two rows of two. Sew the squares into rows. Join the rows to make a four-patch unit measuring 5" square, including seam allowances.

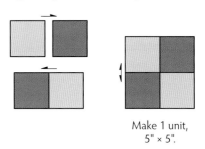

Make 1 unit,
5" × 5".

2. Draw a diagonal line from corner to corner on the wrong side of the beige 2⅜" squares. Layer a marked square on a dark 2⅜" square, right sides together. Sew ¼" from both sides of the drawn

line. Cut the unit apart on the marked line to make two half-square-triangle units. Make 16 units measuring 2" square, including seam allowances.

Make 16 units,
2" × 2".

3. Join three half-square-triangle units to make a row, noting the orientation of the units. Make two rows measuring 2" × 5", including seam allowances.

Make 2 rows,
2" × 5".

4. Join five half-square-triangle units to make a row, noting the orientation of the units. Make two rows measuring 2" × 8", including seam allowances.

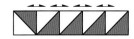

Make 2 rows,
2" × 8".

5. Sew the rows from step 3 to opposite sides of the four-patch unit. Sew the rows from step 4 to the top and bottom of the unit to make a Sawmill block. Repeat the steps to make a total of 18 blocks measuring 8" square, including seam allowances.

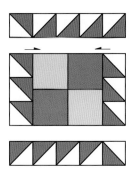 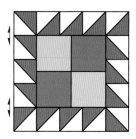

Make 18 blocks,
8" × 8".

Making the Sawmill Side Triangles

For each side triangle, you'll need the following:

- 2 matching beige large triangles
- 4 matching beige 2⅜" squares
- 1 beige small triangle
- 1 dark 2¾" square
- 4 matching dark 2⅜" squares
- 1 dark small triangle

Instructions are for making one side triangle. You'll need 10 total.

1. Sew the short edge of a beige large triangle to one side of the dark 2¾" square. Sew the second beige large triangle to an adjacent side of square.

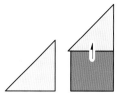 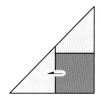

Make 1 unit.

2. Draw a diagonal line from corner to corner on the wrong side of the beige 2⅜" squares. Layer a marked square on a dark 2⅜" square, right sides together. Sew ¼" from both sides of the drawn line. Cut the unit apart on the marked line to make two half-square-triangle units. Make eight units measuring 2" square, including seam allowances. (You'll have one extra unit.)

Make 8 units,
2" × 2".

3. Join three half-square-triangle units to make a row. Sew a dark small triangle to the beige triangle, noting the direction of the dark triangle.

Make 1 row.

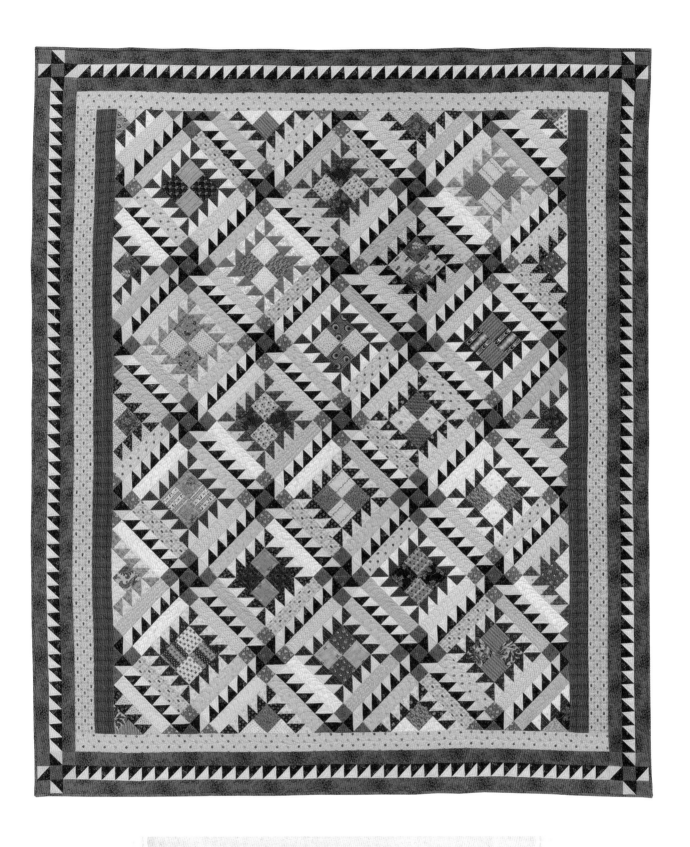

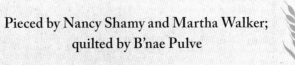

Pieced by Nancy Shamy and Martha Walker;
quilted by B'nae Pulve

4. Join four half-square-triangle units to make a row, noting the direction of the units. Sew a beige small triangle to the dark triangle at one end of the row.

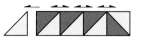

Make 1 row.

5. Sew the row from step 3 to the unit from step 1, noting the orientation of the row. Sew the row from step 4 to the unit to make a Sawmill side triangle. Repeat the steps to make a total of 10 side triangles.

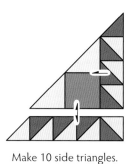

Make 10 side triangles.

Making the Sawmill Corner Triangles

For each corner triangle, you'll need one beige large triangle, one dark large triangle, two matching beige 2⅜" squares, two matching dark 2⅜" squares, one beige small triangle, and one dark small triangle.

1. Sew the beige large triangle to the dark large triangle along one short edge.

Make 1 unit.

2. Referring to step 2 of "Making the Sawmill Side Triangles," use the beige and dark 2⅜" squares to make four half-square-triangle units. (You'll have one extra unit.)

Make 4 units, 2" × 2".

3. Join three half-square-triangle units to make a row. Sew the dark small triangle to the beige end of the row. Sew the beige small triangle to the opposite end of the row. Fold the completed unit in half and finger-press to make a center crease.

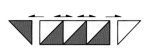
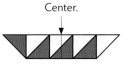

Center.

Make 1 unit.

4. Center and sew the dark-triangle side of the unit from step 3 to the unit from step 1 to make one Sawmill corner triangle. Repeat the steps to make a total of four corner triangles.

Align center.

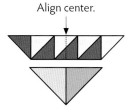
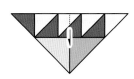

Make 4 corner triangles.

Making the Friendship Star Blocks and Side Triangles

1. Draw a diagonal line from corner to corner on the wrong side of the beige print A 2⅜" squares. Layer a marked square on a brown print A square, right sides together. Sew ¼" from both sides of the drawn line. Cut the unit apart on the marked line to make two half-square-triangle units. Make 112 units measuring 2" square, including seam allowances.

Make 112 units, 2" × 2".

2. Lay out four matching rust 2" squares, four half-square-triangle units, and one red 2" square in three rows of three, noting the orientation of the units. Sew the pieces into rows. Join the rows to make a Friendship Star block. Make 21 blocks measuring 5" square, including seam allowances. You'll use 17 blocks for the quilt center and 4 blocks for the outer border.

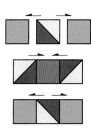

Make 21 blocks, 5" × 5".

WESTWARD HO

In 1870, nearly two-thirds of the state of Missouri was covered in virgin forests, and there were small sawmills throughout the state that furnished lumber to the growing number of homesteaders throughout the Plains region. In the southeast portion of Missouri, tall ancient pine trees forested the Ozarks and were the most valuable timber to be harvested. In 1889, the Grandin Mill in the Ozarks began selling lumber to markets in Nebraska, Kansas, and the Indian Territory, becoming one of the largest mills in the world at that time.

3. Lay out two matching rust triangles, two half-square-triangle units, one red triangle, and one rust square in three rows, noting the orientation of the units and triangles. The rust print should be the same throughout. Sew the pieces into rows. Join rows to make a Friendship Star side triangle. Make 14 side triangles.

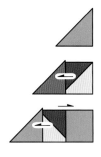
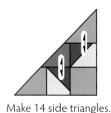

Make 14 side triangles.

Making the Sashing Units and Outer Borders

1. On the wrong side of the cream squares, draw a diagonal line from corner to corner in both directions to form an X. Layer a marked square on top of a brown B square, right sides together. Sew ¼" from both sides of the drawn lines. Cut the units apart horizontally and vertically first. Then cut the units apart on the drawn lines to yield eight half-square-triangle units. Make 416 units measuring 2" square, including seam allowances. You'll use 240 units for sashing and the remaining 176 units for the outer borders.

Make 416 units,
2" × 2".

2. Join five half-square-triangle units, noting the direction of the units. Sew beige rectangles to the top and bottom edges of the triangle row to make a sashing unit. Make 48 sashing units measuring 5" × 8", including seam allowances.

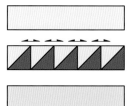

Make 48 units,
5" × 8".

3. Join 48 half-square-triangle units, noting the orientation of the units, to make a side sawtooth border. Make two side borders measuring 2" × 72½", including seam allowances. Join 40 half-square-triangle units, noting the orientation of the units, to make the top sawtooth border measuring 2" × 60½", including seam allowances. Repeat to make the bottom border. Press all seam allowances open.

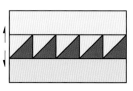

Make 2 side borders,
2" × 72½".

Make 2 top/bottom borders,
2" × 60½".

4. Join 14 rust print 2"-wide strips end to end. From the pieced strip, cut four 72½"-long strips and four 60½"-long strips.

5. Sew a side border from step 3 between two rust 72½"-long strips to make a side outer border. Make two side outer borders measuring 5" × 72½", including seam allowances. Sew the top border from step 3 between two rust 60½"-long strips to make the top outer border measuring 5" × 60½", including seam allowances. Repeat to make the bottom border.

Make 2 side borders,
5" × 72½".

Make 2 top/bottom borders,
5" × 60½".

Assembling the Quilt Top

Refer to the photo on page 25 for placement guidance throughout.

1. Lay out the Sawmill blocks, Sawmill side triangles, Sawmill corner triangles, sashing units, Friendship Star blocks, and Friendship Star triangles in 15 diagonal rows as shown in the quilt assembly diagram below. Sew the pieces into rows. Join the rows to complete the quilt-top center, which should measure 51½" × 68½", including seam allowances.

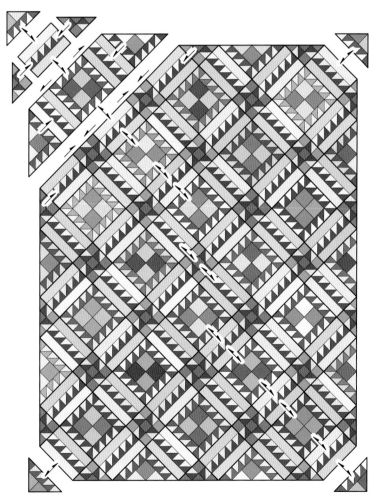

Quilt assembly

the quilt top, again noting the orientation of the brown triangles. The completed quilt top should measure 69½" × 81½".

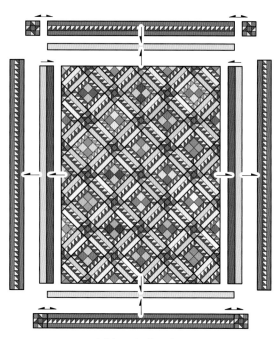

Adding the borders

2. Join the rust plaid strips end to end. Join the beige B strips end to end. From each of the pieced strips, cut two 68½"-long strips.

3. Join a rust plaid strip and a beige B strip along one long edge. Make two and sew them to opposite sides of the quilt top, making sure the rust strip is next to the quilt center. The quilt top should measure 60½" × 68½", including seam allowances.

4. Join the beige C strips end to end. From the pieced strip, cut two 60½"-long strips. Sew the strips to the top and bottom edges of the quilt top. The quilt top should measure 60½" × 72½", including seam allowances.

5. Sew the side outer borders to opposite sides of the quilt top, noting the orientation of the brown triangles. Sew a Friendship Star block to each end of the top and bottom outer borders. Sew these borders to the top and bottom edges of

Finishing the Quilt

For detailed instructions about any of the finishing steps, go to ShopMartingale.com/HowtoQuilt for free, downloadable information.

1. Layer the backing, batting, and quilt top. Baste the layers together.

2. Quilt by hand or machine. The quilt shown is machine quilted with curved lines in the blocks and setting triangles. Half feathers and curved lines are quilted in the sashing units and outer border. Continuous feathers are quilted in the cream middle border, and a continuous motif of diagonal lines and curves is stitched in the rust inner border.

3. Use the remaining rust print 2"-wide strips to make binding, and then attach the binding to the quilt.

Prairie Spring

It was late spring when we left Missouri, and the forests and woodlands through which we traveled were already thick with foliage. After we crossed into Kansas, we continued to ramble through dense stands of hickories, oaks, and colorful redbud trees. After several days, the woodlands gradually gave way to a wide expanse of prairie, with flowers of every color in full bloom.

FINISHED QUILT: 50½" × 71½"

FINISHED BLOCKS: 6" × 12" and 6" × 6"

Materials

Yardage is based on 42"-wide fabric.

⅜ yard of pink print for Prairie Flower and Starflower blocks

2½ yards *total* of assorted beige and light pink prints (referred to collectively as "beige") for Prairie Flower, Postage Stamp, and Sixteen Patch blocks

2¼ yards *total* of assorted brown prints for Prairie Flower, Postage Stamp, Starflower, and Sixteen Patch blocks

⅝ yard of mottled ecru print for Prairie Flower blocks

⅝ yard of light print for Starflower blocks

⅔ yard of tan print for Starflower blocks

¼ yard of beige floral for inner border

2 yards of brown floral for outer border and binding

3¼ yards of fabric for backing

57" × 78" piece of batting

Template plastic

Foundation paper

Chalk marker (optional)

Cutting

Cut all pieces across the width of the fabric unless otherwise noted. All measurements include ¼" seam allowances. Before you begin cutting, trace patterns A–D on pattern sheet 1 onto template plastic and cut them out. Use the templates to cut the A–D pieces from the fabrics indicated below.

From the pink print, cut:

2 strips, 1⅞" × 42"; crosscut into 30 squares, 1⅞" × 1⅞"

1 strip, 1½" × 42"; crosscut into 14 rectangles, 1½" × 2½"

14 of piece D

Continued on page 33

Continued from page 31

From *each* of 4 assorted beige prints, cut:

1 square, 3¼" × 3¼" (4 total)

7 squares, 1½" × 1½" (28 total)

7 rectangles, 2" × 6½" (28 total)

4 rectangles, 1½" × 4½" (16 total; 2 are extra)

4 squares, 1⅞" × 1⅞" (16 total; 2 are extra)

From the remainder of the assorted beige prints, cut a *total* of:

36 strips, 1½" × 22"

32 squares, 1½" × 1½"

From the assorted brown prints, cut a *total* of:

36 strips, 1½" × 22"

14 rectangles, 1½" × 6½"

14 rectangles, 1½" × 4½"

32 squares, 1½" × 1½"

14 sets of 8 matching A pieces

From the mottled ecru print, cut:

13 strips, 1½" × 42"; crosscut into:

    28 rectangles, 1½" × 10½"

    28 rectangles, 1½" × 6½"

From the light print, cut:

112 of piece B

From the tan print, cut:

14 of piece C

From the beige floral, cut:

3 strips, 2" × 42"

From the *lengthwise grain* of the brown floral, cut:

2 strips, 4½" × 63½"

2 strips, 4½" × 42½"

4 strips, 2" × 64"

Prairie Scholars

To learn more about pioneer life, visit ShopMartingale.com/PrairiePatchwork for a bibliography listing the fascinating source material that influenced Carrie's story.

Making the Prairie Flower Blocks

Press seam allowances in the directions indicated by the arrows.

1. Draw a diagonal line from corner to corner on the wrong side of 16 pink 1⅞" squares. Align two squares on opposite corners of a beige 3¼" square, right sides together. The marked squares should overlap in the center. Sew ¼" from both sides of the drawn lines. Cut on the drawn lines to make two units.

2. Place a marked square on the beige corner of a unit from step 1, right sides together and noting the direction of the marked line. Sew ¼" from both sides of the drawn line. Cut the unit apart on the drawn line. Repeat with the remaining marked square and unit from step 1 to yield four flying-geese units. Make a total of 16 flying-geese units measuring 1½" × 2½", including seam allowances. (You'll have two extra units.)

Make 16 units, 1½" × 2½".

3. Draw a diagonal line from corner to corner on the wrong side of the beige 1⅞" squares. Layer a marked square on a pink 1⅞" square, right sides together. Sew ¼" from both sides of the drawn line. Cut the unit apart on the marked line to make two half-square-triangle units. Make 28 units measuring 1½" square, including seam allowances.

Make 28 units, 1½" × 1½".

4. Lay out two beige 1½" squares, one flying-geese unit, two half-square-triangle units, and one pink rectangle in two rows, noting the orientation of the units. The beige print should match in all of the pieces. Sew the pieces into rows. Join the rows to make a flower unit. Make 14 units measuring 2½" × 4½", including seam allowances.

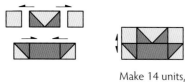

Make 14 units,
2½" × 4½".

5. Sew matching beige 2" × 6½" rectangles to opposite sides of a brown 1½" × 6½" rectangle to make a stem unit. Make 14 units measuring 4½" × 6½", including seam allowances.

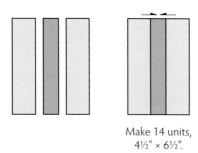

Make 14 units,
4½" × 6½".

6. Lay out one flower unit, one brown 1½" × 4½" rectangle, one stem unit, and one beige 1½" × 4½" rectangle as shown. The beige and brown prints should match in all the pieces. Join the pieces to make a center unit. Make 14 units measuring 4½" × 10½", including seam allowances.

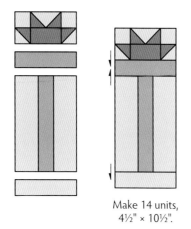

Make 14 units,
4½" × 10½".

7. Sew ecru 1½" × 10½" rectangles to opposite sides of the center unit. Sew ecru 1½" × 6½" rectangles to the top and bottom edges to make a Prairie Flower block. Make 14 blocks measuring 6½" × 12½", including seam allowances.

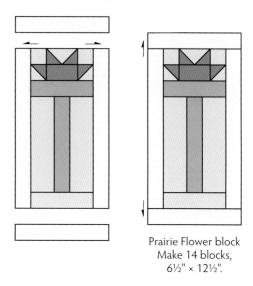

Prairie Flower block
Make 14 blocks,
6½" × 12½".

Making the Postage Stamp Blocks

1. Sew a brown 1½" × 22" strip to each long side of a beige 1½" × 22" strip to make strip set A. Make 12 strip sets measuring 3½" × 22". Crosscut the strip sets into 168 A segments, 1½" × 3½".

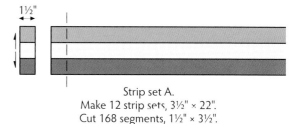

1½"

Strip set A.
Make 12 strip sets, 3½" × 22".
Cut 168 segments, 1½" × 3½".

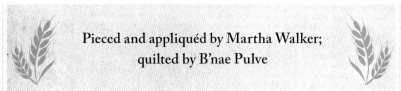

Pieced and appliquéd by Martha Walker;
quilted by B'nae Pulve

3. Join two A segments and one B segment to make a nine-patch unit. Make 56 units measuring 3½" square, including seam allowances.

Make 56 units,
3½" × 3½".

4. Join two B segments and one A segment to make a nine-patch unit. Make 56 units measuring 3½" square, including seam allowances.

Make 56 units,
3½" × 3½".

WESTWARD HO

Likened to a billowing sea by many early travelers through Kansas and the Great Plains, the tall, short, and mixed-grass prairies were also said to have been accompanied by a carpet of flowers of every tint. Prior to the plow, flowers grew more abundantly in hundreds of varieties, such as pink prairie phlox, purple coneflowers, black-eyed Susans, beardtongue, Mead's milkweed, Gayfeathers, blue violets, the eight-foot-tall compass plant, and the now-endangered prairie white-fringed orchid.

2. Sew a beige 1½" × 22" strip to each long side of a brown 1½" × 22" strip to make strip set B. Make 12 strip sets measuring 3½" × 22". Crosscut the strip sets into 168 B segments, 1½" × 3½".

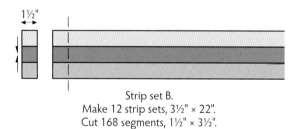

1½"

Strip set B.
Make 12 strip sets, 3½" × 22".
Cut 168 segments, 1½" × 3½".

5. Lay out four units from step 3 and four units from step 4 in four rows of two. Sew the units into rows. Join the rows to make a Postage Stamp block. Make 14 blocks measuring 6½" × 12½", including seam allowances.

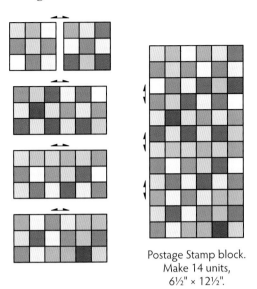

Postage Stamp block.
Make 14 units,
6½" × 12½".

Mix It Up

To create the illusion of randomly scrap-pieced blocks, try this trick. After piecing and cutting the strip sets into segments, place matching segments in a plastic bag; you will have 24 separate bags. Select one segment from each bag, for a total of 24 different A and B segments. Randomly join the selected segments to make the nine-patch units. Then join the units to make a block. Each block will have the same 72 fabrics but with different placements, giving your quilt the illusion of containing more fabrics than it actually does. To add another scrappy element, substitute a few of the strip-pieced segments with units pieced from three totally different 1½" squares.

Making the Starflower Blocks

If you need more information on foundation paper piecing, go to ShopMartingale.com/HowtoQuilt for detailed instructions.

1. Make 28 copies of the foundation pattern on pattern sheet 1.

2. Using eight matching A pieces and eight B pieces, paper piece a total of 14 sets of two matching units (28 total).

3. Trim the paper and fabrics ¼" outside the sewing line on all sides. Join two matching units to make a flower unit.

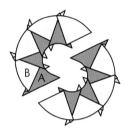

4. Use your favorite appliqué method to mark and cut away the inner circle of fabric piece C for appliqué. Using a chalk marker and pattern C, mark the centering lines on the fabric, or fold piece C in half vertically and horizontally, and lightly crease to establish centering lines. Place piece C on top of a flower unit, matching the center lines and the points on the flower unit. Turn under the seam allowance around the circle opening and appliqué piece C to the flower unit by hand or machine.

5. Appliqué piece D in the center of the flower unit. Center and trim the block to measure 6½" square, including seam allowances. Make 14 Starflower blocks.

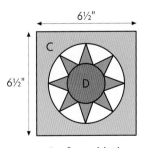

Starflower block.
Make 14 blocks.

Making the Sixteen Patch Blocks

1. Lay out two beige and two brown 1½" squares in two rows of two. Sew the squares into rows. Join the rows to make a four-patch unit. Repeat to make a total of 16 four-patch units.

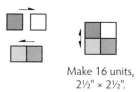

Make 16 units, 2½" × 2½".

2. Lay out four of the four-patch units in two rows of two. Sew the units into rows. Join the rows to make a Sixteen Patch block. Make four blocks measuring 4½" square, including seam allowances.

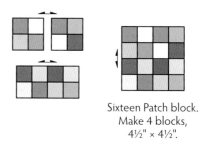

Sixteen Patch block. Make 4 blocks, 4½" × 4½".

Assembling the Quilt Top

1. Lay out the Prairie Flower and Postage Stamp blocks in four rows of seven blocks each, alternating the blocks in each row as shown in the quilt assembly diagram on page 39. Sew the blocks into rows. Join the rows to make the quilt-top center, which should measure 42½" × 48½", including seam allowances.

2. Join the beige floral 2"-wide strips end to end. From the pieced strip, cut two 42½"-long strips. Sew the strips to the top and bottom edges of the quilt top. The quilt top should measure 42½" × 51½", including seam allowances.

3. Join seven Starflower blocks to make a row measuring 6½" × 42½", including seam allowances. Repeat to make a second row. Sew the rows to the top and bottom edges of the quilt top. The quilt top should measure 42½" × 63½", including seam allowances.

4. Sew the brown floral 4½" × 63½" strips to opposite sides of the quilt top.

5. Sew a Sixteen Patch block to each end of the brown floral 4½" × 42½" strips, and sew them to the top and bottom edges of the quilt top. The completed quilt top should measure 50½" × 71½".

Finishing the Quilt

For detailed instructions about any of the finishing steps, go to ShopMartingale.com/HowtoQuilt for free, downloadable information.

1. Layer the backing, batting, and quilt top. Baste the layers together.

2. Quilt by hand or machine. The quilt shown is machine quilted with swirls and feathers in the Prairie Flower blocks and curved lines in the Postage Stamp blocks. Evenly spaced straight lines are quilted throughout the inner border. The Starflower blocks are quilted with curved lines around the star points, a feather motif in the center circles, and swirls between the large circles. A continuous feather is quilted in the outer border and curved lines are stitched in the Sixteen Patch blocks.

3. Use the brown floral 2"-wide strips to make binding, and then attach the binding to the quilt.

Quilt assembly

Pipe Creek

In Kansas we claimed a spot near Pipe Creek, as we wanted to be near water. Seeing several prairie fires on our way from Missouri had made us mindful of water's importance for our safety, and we would also need water close at hand for personal use until we could dig a well. Aunt and Uncle claimed a nearby spot along the creek. A great many other families are also living along the creek, which stretches for miles. Before we had a well, I made frequent trips to the creek for water and became quite acquainted with the different plants that grew along its banks.

FINISHED QUILT: 32½" × 32½"
FINISHED BLOCKS: 12" × 12" and 2" × 3"

Materials

Yardage is based on 42"-wide fabric. Fat quarters are 18" × 21"; fat eighths are 9" × 21"; and fat sixteenths are 9" × 10½".

COTTON

1¼ yards of black tone on tone for blocks and binding

½ yard *total* of assorted red prints for border blocks

1 fat quarter of red floral for sashing

1 fat sixteenth of cheddar orange print for sashing

1 fat sixteenth of olive green print for sashing and border

1⅛ yards of fabric for backing

WOOL

1 fat quarter of olive green A for leaf and star appliqués

1 fat quarter of olive green B for leaf appliqués

1 fat quarter of red for star, circle, and stem appliqués

1 fat eighth of gold for circle and stem appliqués

1 square, 5" × 5", of gold houndstooth for circle appliqués

OTHER MATERIALS

37" × 37" square of batting

Freezer paper

#24 chenille needle

Tapestry needle threader

Chalk wheel

WOOL THREAD

Select thread colors to coordinate with wool colors. Colors listed below are for Aurifil Lana wool thread.

- Brick Red (8265) for stars, circles, and stems
- Gold (8142) for circles and stems
- Gray Green (8930) for leaves
- Leaf Green (8950) for leaves and stars

Pieced and appliquéd by Martha Walker; quilted by B'nae Pulve

Cutting

Cut all pieces across the width of the fabric unless otherwise noted.

From the black tone on tone, cut:

2 strips, 13½" × 42"; crosscut into:
    4 squares, 13½" × 13½"
    30 rectangles, 2½" × 3½"

2 strips, 2½" × 42"; crosscut into 22 rectangles, 2½" × 3½"

4 strips, 2" × 42"

From the assorted red prints, cut a *total* of:

208 squares, 1½" × 1½"

From the red floral, cut:

4 rectangles, 2½" × 12½"

From the cheddar orange print, cut:

8 squares, 1½" × 1½"

From the olive green print, cut:

4 squares, 3½" × 3½"

1 square, 2½" × 2½"

Make It Easy

Plastic or acrylic stencil sheets that have circle cutouts ranging in diameter from ¹⁄₁₆" to 2¼" are available in office-supply stores in the architectural drafting section, in art-supply stores, and at some hobby shops. This type of stencil makes it easy to quickly trace circles onto freezer paper for wool or cotton appliqué. Simply match the circle size on the patterns provided to a circle on the stencil.

Appliquéing the Blocks

Go to ShopMartingale.com/HowtoQuilt for detailed embroidery instructions as needed.

1. Referring to the appliqué patterns on pattern sheet 1, trace each shape onto the dull side of the freezer paper the number of times indicated on the pattern. Using a warm iron, press the freezer-paper templates onto the wool in the colors indicated, shiny side down. Cut out each shape on the traced line.

2. Center a red stem on an olive green leaf, positioning the stem approximately 1¾" from the tip of the leaf. Thread baste the stem in place. Whipstitch the edge of the stem using two strands of Brick Red thread. Make 16 leaves.

3. Referring to the appliqué placement diagram on page 43, pin seven red small circles on each leaf. Whipstitch the circles in place using two strands of Brick Red thread.

4. Pin a gold houndstooth circle in the center of a red large circle. Use two strands of Gold thread to blanket stitch the gold circle to the red circle. Make four center units.

5. Using a chalk wheel, mark vertical and horizontal lines through the center of a black 13½" square. Position a gold stem on each marked line, approximately 1⅛" from the outer edges of the square. Thread baste each rectangle in place, then whipstitch the stem in place using two strands of Gold. Make four blocks.

6. Draw diagonal lines on a block from corner to corner in both directions using a chalk wheel. Using the diagonal guidelines, center two olive green A leaves and two olive green B leaves from step 3 between each gold stem, alternating the leaf colors. The tips of the leaves should meet in the center of the black square. Blanket stitch the leaves using two strands of Gray Green or Leaf Green thread to match the leaves. Make four blocks.

7. Position a center unit in the center of each block. Place a red star on the end of each gold stem. Use two strands of Brick Red thread to blanket stitch around each shape. Make four blocks.

8. Trim each block to 12½" square, keeping the design centered.

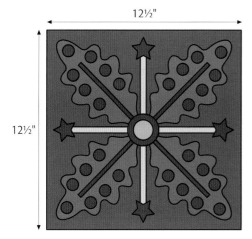

Appliqué placement

Making the Appliquéd Border

Press seam allowances in the directions indicated by the arrows.

1. Draw a diagonal line from corner to corner on the wrong side of the red print 1½" squares. Place marked squares on opposite corners of a black rectangle. Sew on the marked lines. Trim the excess corner fabric ¼" from the stitched line. Place marked squares on the remaining corners of the rectangle. Sew, trim, and press as before to make a border block. Make 52 blocks measuring 2½" × 3½", including seam allowances.

Make 52 blocks,
2½" × 3½".

2. Join 13 blocks to make a border strip. Make four border strips measuring 3½" × 26½", including seam allowances.

Make 4 borders,
3½" × 26½".

3. Whipstitch a red small circle in the center of a gold medium circle using two strands of Brick Red thread. Make a total of 24 penny units.

4. To make a side border, center four green stars, three red stars, and six penny units on the blocks in one border strip, alternating the shapes as shown in the quilt assembly diagram on page 45. Blanket stitch the shapes in place using two strands of thread to match the wool shapes. Repeat to make a second side border.

5. To make the top border, center four red stars, three green stars, and six penny units on the blocks in one of the remaining border strips, alternating the shapes as shown below. Blanket stitch the shapes in place using two strands of thread to match the wool shapes. Repeat to make the bottom border.

6. Sew an olive green 3½" square to each end of the border strips from step 5. The top and bottom borders should now measure 3½" × 32½", including seam allowances.

Make 2 top/bottom borders,
3½" × 32½".

Assembling the Quilt Top

1. Draw a diagonal line from corner to corner on the wrong side of the cheddar orange squares. Place a marked square on one corner of a red floral rectangle, right sides together. Sew on the marked line. Trim the excess corner fabric ¼" from the stitched line. Place a marked square on the adjacent corner of the rectangle. Sew and trim as before to make a sashing strip. Make four strips measuring 2½" × 12½", including seam allowances.

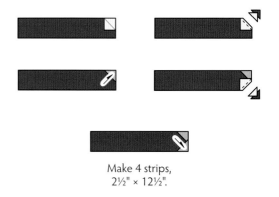

Make 4 strips,
2½" × 12½".

2. Lay out the appliquéd blocks, sashing units, and olive green 2½" square in three rows as shown in the quilt assembly diagram on page 45. Sew the pieces into rows. Then join the rows to complete the quilt-top center, which should measure 26½" square, including seam allowances.

WESTWARD HO

The homesteaders had to ensure themselves a water supply in a land that often lay bone-dry despite torrential spring rains. Some settlers collected rain in barrels and cisterns; others relied on water from a creek if one ran nearby.

3. Sew the appliquéd side borders to opposite sides of the quilt top. Sew the top and bottom borders to the top and bottom edges. The completed quilt top should measure 32½" square.

Finishing the Quilt

For detailed instructions about any of the finishing steps, go to ShopMartingale.com/HowtoQuilt for free, downloadable information.

1. Layer the backing, batting, and quilt top. Baste the layers together.

2. Quilt by hand or machine. The quilt shown is machine quilted in the ditch around the appliqué shapes, and swirls are quilted in the appliquéd blocks. Curved lines are quilted in the border blocks, and evenly spaced straight lines are quilted throughout the sashing strips. The border squares and center square feature a feather motif.

3. Use the black 2"-wide strips to make binding, and then attach the binding to the quilt.

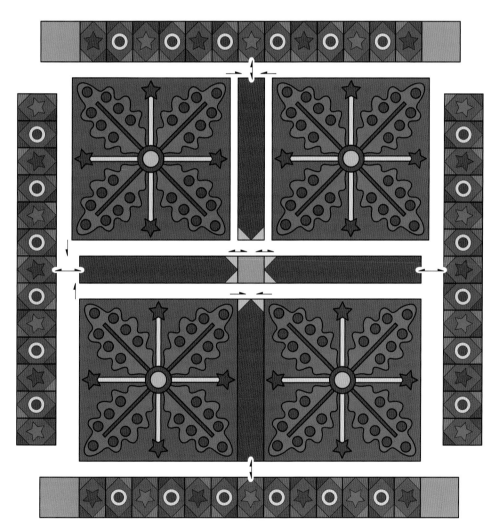

Quilt assembly

Sunflower Fields

I missed the Allegheny Mountains that surrounded our old Virginia home. The highest point near our homestead in Kansas is a large hill called Buzzard's Roost. Eliza, cousin Mary, and I would sometimes climb to the top and gaze down at the prairie, which was frequently blanketed by a profusion of sunflowers.

FINISHED QUILT: 72¾" × 72¾"
FINISHED BLOCK: 12" × 12"

Materials

Yardage is based on 42"-wide fabric. Fat quarters are 18" × 21"; fat eighths are 9" × 21".

28 fat eighths of assorted light prints for blocks

12 fat eighths of assorted blue prints for blocks

10 fat eighths of assorted red prints for blocks

3 fat eighths of assorted brown prints for blocks

4 squares, 4" × 4", of assorted black prints for blocks

⅝ yard of red print A for blocks, setting triangles, and border squares

1 yard *total* of assorted beige and cream prints (referred to collectively as "beige") for blocks and border squares

¼ yard of blue plaid for setting triangles

2⅜ yards of navy print for sashing, border 3, and binding

1 fat eighth of red print B for sashing squares and triangles

2⅛ yards of beige floral for setting triangles and borders 2 and 4

1⅞ yards of black print for border 1

4½ yards of fabric for backing

79" × 79" square of batting

Template plastic

Cutting

Before you begin cutting, trace the complete outline of patterns A–F on pattern sheet 1 onto template plastic and cut them out. Use the templates to draw the shapes onto the wrong side of the fabrics indicated, and then cut out the fabric pieces, being sure to add a ¼" seam allowance to each shape. Cut all pieces across the width of the fabric unless otherwise noted. Measurements for all other pieces include seam allowances.

From the assorted light fat eighths, cut a *total* of:

12 sets of 9 matching A pieces

1 set of 9 matching B pieces

12 sets of 9 matching C pieces

3 sets of 4 matching D pieces

1 of piece E

From the assorted blue fat eighths, cut a *total* of:

1 set of 9 matching A pieces

7 sets of 9 matching B pieces

4 sets of 4 matching D pieces

2 of piece E

From the assorted red fat eighths, cut a *total* of:

5 sets of 9 matching B pieces

1 set of 9 matching C pieces

3 sets of 4 matching D pieces

6 of piece E

Continued on page 48

Continued from page 47

From *each* of the black 4" squares, cut:

1 of piece E (4 total)

From *each* of the brown fat eighths, cut:

3 sets of 4 matching D pieces

From the assorted beige prints, cut a *total* of:

13 sets of 4 matching F pieces

13 sets of 4 matching squares, 2" × 2"

1 set of 8 matching squares, 2" × 2"

13 sets of 4 matching rectangles, 2" × 6½"

From red print A, cut:

9 strips, 2" × 42"; crosscut into 164 squares, 2" × 2"

From the blue plaid, cut:

4 strips, 2" × 42"; crosscut into 20 rectangles,
2" × 6½"

From the *lengthwise grain* of the navy print, cut:

10 strips, 2" × 75"; crosscut *6 of the strips* into 36
rectangles, 2" × 12½"

4 strips, 3½" × 63¾"

From red print B, cut:

2 strips, 2" × 21"; crosscut into 12 squares, 2" × 2"

3 squares, 3⅜" × 3⅜"; cut the squares into quarters
diagonally to yield 12 triangles

From the *lengthwise grain* of the beige floral cut:

4 strips, 2" × 69¾"

4 strips, 2" × 60¾"

2 squares, 9¾" × 9¾"; cut the squares into quarters
diagonally to yield 8 large triangles

2 squares, 5¼" × 5¼"; cut the squares in half
diagonally to yield 4 corner triangles

12 squares, 3⅜" × 3⅜"; cut the squares into quarters
diagonally to yield 48 small triangles

20 rectangles, 2" × 6½"

16 squares, 2" × 2"

From the *lengthwise grain* of the black print, cut:

4 strips, 2" × 57¾"

Making the Sunflower Blocks

For each block, select one set of pieces A–F, referring to the photo on page 49 for placement guidance. The following instructions are for hand piecing the Sunflower petal unit. You can machine piece the unit if desired. Machine piecing instructions are given for piecing the remainder of the Sunflower block and quilt. Press seam allowances in the directions indicated by the arrows. Use your favorite appliqué method to prepare and appliqué pieces E and F.

1. Using a small running stitch, sew a B piece to an A piece along the marked seam line, starting and ending with a backstitch. Make nine units.

Backstitch.

Make 9 units.

2. Sew a C piece to the opposite side of B as shown to make an A/B/C unit. Make nine units.

Backstitch.   Make 9 units.

3. Join the units to make a petal unit. When hand piecing, sew only on the marked seamlines, leaving the seam allowances free to be pressed to either side. Repeat the steps to make a total of 13 units.

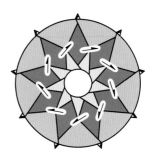

Make 13 units.

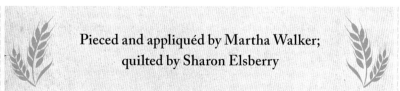
Pieced and appliquéd by Martha Walker;
quilted by Sharon Elsberry

4. Join two D pieces along one short edge. Make two. Sew the units together to make the background unit. Repeat to make a total of 13 units.

Make 2 units.

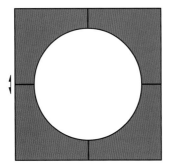

Make 13 units.

WESTWARD HO

Sunflowers grow in every Kansas county because they are so adaptable to a variety of soil types such as sand and clay, and they can also tolerate dry to medium-moist soils. The state is home to 12 different species, including both annual and perennial varieties. Early settlers burned the sunflower stalks for fuel and fed the seeds to their poultry. Sunflowers are also an important source of food for birds and small mammals.

5. With right sides together, pin a petal unit on top of a background unit, aligning the raw edges and matching one of the B points to one of the seamlines on the background. On the opposite side of the petal unit, match the center of the A piece to the seamline. Sew the petal unit to the background unit, easing each half of the petal unit between the two seamlines.

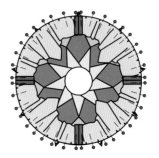

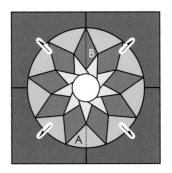

6. Appliqué the E circle in the center of the petal unit. Position an F piece on each corner of the background unit, aligning the outer edges. Turn under the two inside edges and then appliqué them to the background. Make 13 sunflower units measuring 9½" square, including seam allowances.

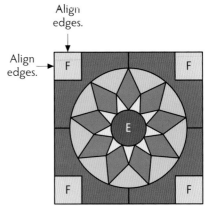

Make 13 units,
9½" × 9½".

7. Sew a red print A square to each end of a beige print 2" × 6½" rectangle. Make 13 sets of four matching units measuring 2" × 9½", including seam allowances.

Make 13 sets of 4 matching units,
2" × 9½".

8. Lay out four matching beige print 2" squares, four matching units from step 7, and one sunflower unit in three rows. The beige squares should match the F pieces in the Sunflower unit. Sew the pieces into rows. Join the rows to make a Sunflower block. Make a total of 13 blocks measuring 12½" square, including seam allowances.

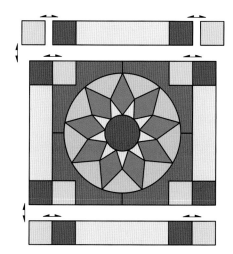

Sunflower block.
Make 13 blocks,
12½" × 12½".

Making the Setting Triangles

1. Sew the short edge of a beige floral small triangle to a red print A square. Sew a second beige small triangle to an adjacent side of the square. Make 24 units.

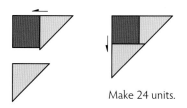

Make 24 units.

2. Join a beige floral rectangle and a blue plaid rectangle along their long edges. Make 20 units measuring 3½" × 6½", including seam allowances.

Make 20 units,
3½" × 6½".

3. Sew a unit from step 1 to each end of a unit from step 2. Sew the long edge of a beige floral corner triangle to the top of the unit to make a corner unit. Make four corner units.

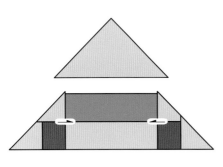

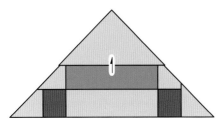

Make 4 corner units.

4. Lay out two red print A and two beige floral 2" squares in two rows of two. Sew the squares into rows. Join the rows to make a four-patch unit. Make eight units measuring 3½" square, including seam allowances.

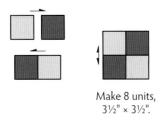

Make 8 units,
3½" × 3½".

5. Sew a four-patch unit to the left end of a unit from step 2. Sew a unit from step 1 to the right end of the unit. Make eight units.

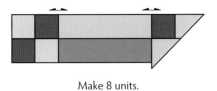

Make 8 units.

6. Sew a unit from step 2 to the short edge of a beige floral large triangle. Make eight units.

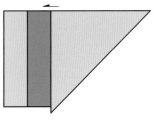

Make 8 units.

7. Join a unit from step 5 to the top of a unit from step 6. Sew a unit from step 1 to the bottom of the unit from step 6 to make a side triangle. Make eight side triangles.

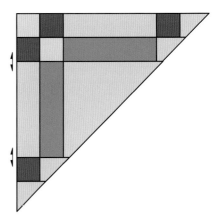

Make 8 side triangles.

Assembling the Quilt Top

1. Lay out the Sunflower blocks, side triangles, corner units, navy rectangles, red print B squares and triangles in 13 diagonal rows as shown in the quilt assembly diagram below. Sew the pieces into rows. Join the rows to complete the quilt-top center, which should measure 57¾" square, including seam allowances.

2. Sew black strips to opposite sides of the quilt-top center. Sew red print A squares to the ends of the remaining black strips. Sew these strips to the top and bottom edges of the quilt top. The quilt top should measure 60¾" square, including seam allowances.

3. Sew beige floral 2" × 60¾" strips to opposite sides of the quilt top. Sew red print A squares to the ends of the remaining beige floral 2" × 60¾" strips. Sew these strips to the top and bottom edges of the quilt top. The quilt top should measure 63¾" square, including seam allowances.

4. Lay out two red print A and two beige print 2" squares in two rows of two. Sew the squares into rows. Join the rows to make a Four Patch block. Make four blocks measuring 3½" square, including seam allowances.

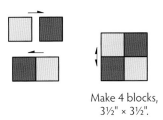

Make 4 blocks,
3½" × 3½".

5. Sew navy 3½" × 63¾" strips to opposite sides of the quilt top. Sew the Four Patch blocks to the ends of the remaining navy strips. Sew these strips to the top and bottom of the quilt top. The quilt top should measure 69¾" square, including seam allowances.

Quilt assembly

6. Sew beige floral 2" × 69¾" strips to opposite sides of the quilt top. Sew red print A squares to the ends of the remaining beige floral 2" × 69¾" strips. Sew these strips to the top and bottom edges of the quilt top. The completed quilt top should measure 72¾" square.

Finishing the Quilt

For detailed instructions about any of the finishing steps, go to ShopMartingale.com/HowtoQuilt for free, downloadable information.

1. Layer the backing, batting, and quilt top. Baste the layers together.

2. Quilt by hand or machine. The quilt shown is machine quilted with curved lines, loops, and swirls in the quilt center. A feather motif is quilted in the side and corner triangles. Curved lines are quilted in the black border. Feathers are quilted in the navy border and continuous loops are stitched in the beige borders.

3. Use the remaining navy 2"-wide strips to make binding, and then attach the binding to the quilt.

Adding the borders

Church Picnic

In July, we had a great picnic to raise money for construction of our church. Makeshift tables were brought to the future church site and laid out with food items donated by our families. We all had a grand time.

FINISHED QUILT: 60½" × 60½"

FINISHED BLOCKS: 12" × 27", 12" × 12", and 3" × 3"

Materials

Yardage is based on 42"-wide fabric. Fat quarters are 18" × 21"; fat eighths are 9" × 21".

¾ yard *total* of assorted teal prints for Nine Patch blocks and appliqués

1¼ yards *total* of assorted cream prints for Nine Patch blocks and dogtooth borders

1¾ yards of beige print A for corner blocks, appliqués, and middle border

1⅝ yards of cream tone on tone for side blocks and appliqués

1 fat quarter *each* of gold and brown prints for appliqués

1 fat eighth *each* of 2 different red prints for appliqués

1 fat quarter of blue plaid for appliqués

1 fat eighth of aqua print for appliqués

1 square, 6" × 6", of black print for appliqués

⅜ yard of beige print B for appliqués and setting squares

1¼ yards of dark teal tone on tone for dogtooth borders and binding

3¾ yards of fabric for backing

67" × 67" square of batting

Freezer paper

Cutting

Use your favorite appliqué technique to prepare the appliqué pieces on pattern sheet 2 for the corner and side blocks. The patterns are reversed for fusible appliqué or freezer-paper appliqué where the freezer paper is ironed to the wrong side of the fabrics. Use the cutting instructions noted on each piece. Cut all pieces below across the width of the fabric unless otherwise noted. All measurements include ¼" seam allowances.

From the assorted teal prints, cut a *total* of:

16 strips, 1¼" × 10½"

8 strips, 2" × 8½"

From the assorted cream prints, cut a *total* of:

16 strips, 1¼" × 8½"

8 strips, 2" × 10½"

176 squares, 2⅜" × 2⅜"

Continued on page 57

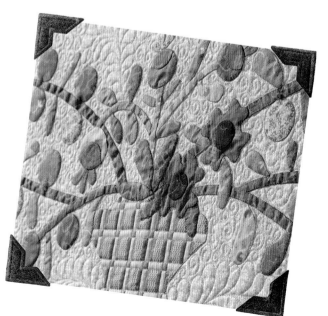

Continued from page 55

From beige print A, cut from the *lengthwise* grain:

2 strips, 2" × 54½"

2 strips, 2" × 57½"

From the remainder of beige print A, cut:

4 squares, 12½" × 12½"

From the cream tone on tone, cut:

4 strips, 12½" × 42"; crosscut into 4 rectangles,
  12½" × 27½"

From beige print B, cut:

3 strips, 3½" × 42"; crosscut into 32 squares,
  3½" × 3½"

From the dark teal tone on tone, cut:

5 strips, 4¼" × 42"; crosscut into 44 squares,
  4¼" × 4¼"

8 strips, 2" × 42"; crosscut *1 of the strips* into
  12 squares, 2" × 2"

Making the Nine Patch Blocks

Press seam allowances in the directions indicated
by the arrows.

1. Join two teal 1¼" × 10½" strips and one cream
  2" × 10½" strip along the long edges to make
  strip set A. Make eight strip sets measuring
  3½" × 10½", including seam allowances.
  Crosscut the strip sets into 64 A segments,
  1¼" × 3½".

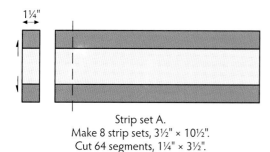

Strip set A.
Make 8 strip sets, 3½" × 10½".
Cut 64 segments, 1¼" × 3½".

2. Join two cream 1¼" × 8½" strips and one teal
  2" × 8½" strip along the long edges to make
  strip set B. Make eight strip sets measuring
  3½" × 8½", including seam allowances. Crosscut
  the strip sets into 32 B segments, 2" × 3½".

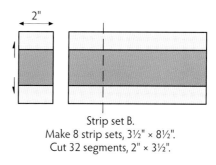

Strip set B.
Make 8 strip sets, 3½" × 8½".
Cut 32 segments, 2" × 3½".

3. Join A segments to both long edges of a
  B segment to make a Nine Patch block. Make
  32 blocks measuring 3½" square, including seam
  allowances.

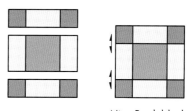

Nine Patch block.
Make 32 blocks,
3½" × 3½".

**ieced and appliquéd by Martha Walker;
  quilted by B'nae Pulve**

Appliquéing the Blocks

Refer to the photos on pages 56 and 59 for placement guidance throughout.

1. Referring to the appliqué placement guide below, pin or glue baste appliqué pieces A–J right side up on a beige print A square, starting with the bottommost layer of appliqué pieces and working in alphabetical order toward the topmost layer of pieces. Use your favorite method to appliqué the pieces in place. Make four corner blocks.

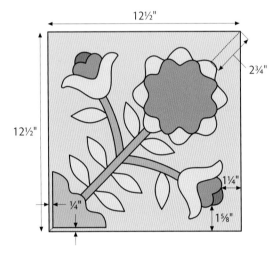

Corner block appliqué placement guide

2. Referring to the appliqué placement guide below, pin or glue baste the appliqué pieces right side up on a cream tone-on-tone rectangle, starting with the bottommost layer of appliqué pieces (stems and leaves) and working toward the topmost layer pieces. Appliqué the pieces in place. Make four side blocks.

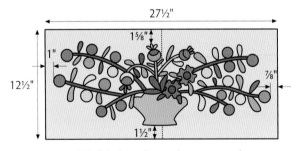

Side block appliqué placement guide

Positioning the Appliqués

There are many ways to place appliqué shapes accurately onto a background. For simple or symmetrical designs, fold the background in half vertically and horizontally and lightly crease. Fold diagonally in both directions and lightly crease again to make no-mark guides for placing the shapes.

For more complicated designs, a light box is helpful. For the larger appliqué blocks in this project, I had an 18" x 36" piece of Plexiglas cut at my local hardware store, and that allowed enough room on either side to prop it up on boxes with a light underneath.

Making the Dogtooth Borders

1. Draw a diagonal line from corner to corner on the wrong side of each cream 2⅜" square. Align two squares on opposite corners of a dark teal 4¼" square, right sides together. The marked squares should overlap in the center. Sew ¼" from both sides of the drawn lines. Cut on the drawn lines to make two units.

2. Place a marked square on the dark teal corner of a unit from step 1, right sides together and noting the direction of the marked line. Sew ¼" from both sides of the drawn line. Cut the unit apart on the drawn line. Repeat with the remaining marked square and unit from step 1 to yield four flying-geese units. Make a total of 176 flying-geese units measuring 2" × 3½", including seam allowances.

Make 176 units,
2" × 3½".

3. Join eight flying-geese units to make a side border that measures 2" × 24½", including seam allowances. Make four. Add a dark teal 2" square to each end of two of the borders. The top and bottom borders should measure 2" × 27½", including seam allowances.

Make 2 side borders,
2" × 24½".

Make 2 top/bottom borders,
2" × 27½".

4. Join 17 flying-geese units to make a side border measuring 2" × 51½", including seam allowances. Make four. Add a dark teal 2" square to each end of two of the borders. The top and bottom borders should measure 2" × 54½", including seam allowances.

Make 2 side borders,
2" × 51½".

Make 2 top/bottom borders,
2" × 54½".

5. Join 19 flying-geese units to make a side border measuring 2" × 57½", including seam allowances. Make four. Add a dark teal 2" square to each end. The top and bottom borders should measure 2" × 60½", including seam allowances.

Make 2 side borders,
2" × 57½".

Make 2 top/bottom borders,
2" × 60½".

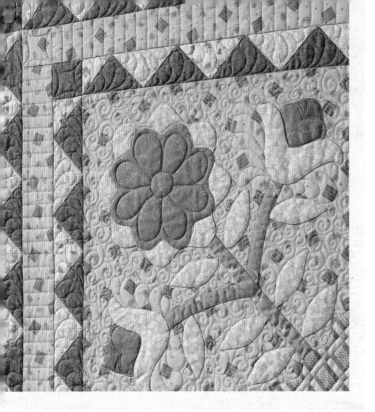

Assembling the Quilt Top

1. Lay out the Nine Patch blocks and beige print B squares in eight rows of eight, alternating the blocks and squares as shown in the quilt assembly diagram. Sew the blocks and squares into rows. Join the rows to make the quilt-top center, which should measure 24½" square, including seam allowances.

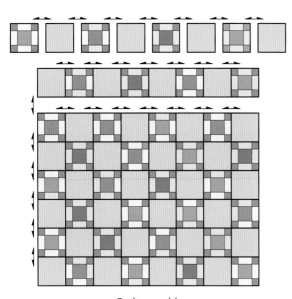

Quilt assembly

WESTWARD HO

A community cemetery had existed on the Thomas Murphy homestead in Kansas since 1870. In 1886, Mahala and Thomas Murphy deeded the land to the Diocese of Leavenworth for a permanent Catholic Cemetery. Also at that time, Henry and Elizabeth Richard deeded land across the road so that a church could be built for the families who lived in Pipe Creek, Meredith Township. Subscription proceeds from the congregation netted $676.50, and a parish social netted $57.00, which made up their building fund. The congregations purchased materials from local companies and furnished the labor. Prior to Saint Peter's Church being completed, various members of the congregation opened their homes for worship services and to house the priest during his arduous trips throughout the settlements.

2. With the teal triangles pointing toward the quilt center, sew the 24½"-long dogtooth borders to opposite sides of the quilt-top center. Sew the 27½"-long dogtooth borders to the top and bottom edges. The quilt top should measure 27½" square, including seam allowances.

3. Sew appliquéd side blocks to opposite sides of the quilt center, making sure the baskets of flowers face away from the quilt center. Sew appliquéd corner blocks to the ends of each remaining side block, noting the orientation

of the blocks in the diagram below. Make two and sew them to the top and bottom edges of the quilt center. The quilt top should measure 51½" square, including seam allowances.

4. With the teal triangles pointing away from the quilt center, sew the 51½"-long dogtooth borders to opposite sides of the quilt-top center. Sew the 54½"-long dogtooth borders to the top and bottom edges. The quilt top should measure 54½" square, including seam allowances.

5. Sew beige print A 2" × 54½" strips to opposite sides of the quilt top. Sew beige print A 2" × 57½" strips to the top and bottom edges. The quilt top should measure 57½" square, including seam allowances.

6. With the teal triangles pointing away from the quilt center, sew the 57½"-long dogtooth borders to opposite sides of the quilt top. Sew the 60½"-long dogtooth borders to the top and bottom edges. The completed quilt top should measure 60½" square.

Finishing the Quilt

For detailed instructions about any of the finishing steps, go to ShopMartingale.com/HowtoQuilt for free, downloadable information.

1. Layer the backing, batting, and quilt top. Baste the layers together.

2. Quilt by hand or machine. The quilt shown is machine quilted with curved lines in the setting squares and stitched in the ditch in the Nine Patch blocks. Feathers are quilted in the triangles of all the dogtooth borders, and evenly spaced straight lines are quilted in the beige border. The appliquéd blocks feature a combination of feathers and swirls, with outline quilting around the appliqués.

3. Use the dark teal 2"-wide strips to make binding, and then attach the binding to the quilt.

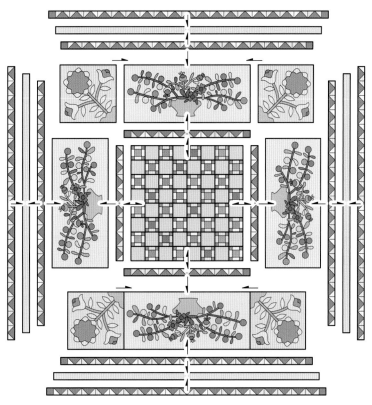

Adding the borders

Ma's Sewing Basket

It was such fun to borrow Ma's sewing basket of scraps, needles, and thread to piece together patches for my own quilts. My first quilt was a little Nine Patch design for my china doll, made with small squares of indigos and shirtings.

FINISHED QUILT: 30½" × 36½"

FINISHED BLOCK: 6" × 6"

Materials

Yardage is based on 42"-wide fabric. Fat quarters are 18" × 21"; fat sixteenths are 9" × 10½".

½ yard *total* of assorted teal prints for blocks

½ yard *total* of assorted cream prints for blocks

½ yard of aqua print for blocks and inner border

⅝ yard of red print #1 for blocks, pieced border, and binding

1 fat quarter of red print #2 for blocks, sashing squares, and pieced border

1 fat sixteenth of gold print for blocks

¼ yard of teal print for pieced border

½ yard of cream print #1 for sashing

⅓ yard of cream print #2 for pieced border

1¼ yards of fabric for backing

37" × 43" rectangle of batting

Template plastic

Cutting

Cut all pieces across the width of the fabric unless otherwise noted. All measurements include ¼" seam allowances. Note that pieces are labeled A–D, indicating their position within each scrappy patchwork block. Before you begin cutting, trace pattern D on pattern sheet 1 onto template plastic and cut it out. Use the template to draw the square onto the wrong side of the fabrics indicated below, and then cut out the D squares. Use your favorite appliqué method to prepare the basket handle on pattern sheet 1 for appliqué.

From the assorted teal prints, cut a *total* of:

12 rectangles, 3½" × 6½" (A)

6 squares, 4¼" × 4¼"; cut the squares into quarters diagonally to yield 24 triangles (B)

1 square, 2¾" × 2¾"; cut the square into quarters diagonally to yield 4 triangles (C; 2 are extra)

5 of piece D

From the assorted cream prints, cut a *total* of:

9 squares, 4¼" × 4¼"; cut the squares into quarters diagonally to yield 36 triangles (B; 3 are extra)

10 basket handles

1 square, 2¾" × 2¾"; cut the square into quarters diagonally to yield 4 triangles (C)

6 of piece D

Continued on page 64

Continued on page 64

Pieced and appliquéd by Martha Walker; quilted by Sharon Elsberry

Continued from page 63

From the aqua print, cut:

2 strips, 2½" × 30¾"

2 strips, 1⅞" × 27½"

1 square, 4¼" × 4¼"; cut the square into quarters diagonally to yield 4 triangles (B; 1 is extra)

2 squares, 2¾" × 2¾"; cut the squares into quarters diagonally to yield 8 triangles (C; 2 are extra)

2 basket handles

6 of piece D

From red print #1, cut:

2 strips, 4¼" × 42"; crosscut into:

　10 squares, 4¼" × 4¼"

　8 squares, 2¾" × 2¾"; cut the squares into quarters diagonally to yield 32 triangles (C)

1 of piece D

4 strips, 2" × 42"

From red print #2, cut:

5 squares, 2¾" × 2¾"; cut the squares into quarters diagonally to yield 20 triangles (C)

7 of piece D

20 squares, 1¾" × 1¾"

4 squares, 2" × 2"

From the gold print, cut:

2 squares, 2¾" × 2¾"; cut the squares into quarters diagonally to yield 8 triangles (C)

11 of piece D

From the teal print for dogtooth border, cut:

3 strips, 2⅜" × 42"; crosscut into 40 squares, 2⅜" × 2⅜"

From cream print #1, cut:

2 strips, 6½" × 42"; crosscut into 31 rectangles, 1¾" × 6½"

From cream print #2, cut:

5 strips, 2" × 42"; crosscut into 80 squares, 2" × 2"

Making the Basket Blocks

Referring to the photo on page 62 for placement guidance, divide the A–D pieces into 12 sets. Instructions are for making one block, using one set of A–D pieces and one basket handle. You'll need 12 blocks total. Press seam allowances in the directions indicated by the arrows.

1. Fold the A rectangle in half lengthwise and finger-press to mark the center crease. Fold the basket handle in half and lightly finger-press the center crease. Place the basket handle on the rectangle, matching the center creases and aligning the raw edges. Use your favorite method to appliqué the handle in place.

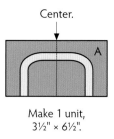

Center.

Make 1 unit,
3½" × 6½".

2. Join one teal B triangle that matches the A rectangle and one cream or aqua B triangle along their short edges. Make one unit. Reverse the orientation of the colors to make one reversed unit.

Make 1 of each unit.

3. Sew the short edge of a C triangle to a D square. Sew a matching C triangle to an adjacent side of the square. Make three units. (Referring to the photo on page 62, note that the base of the basket in each block has two matching units. For most of the blocks, the fabrics in the unit in the center of the basket are the reverse of the base units.)

Make 3 units.

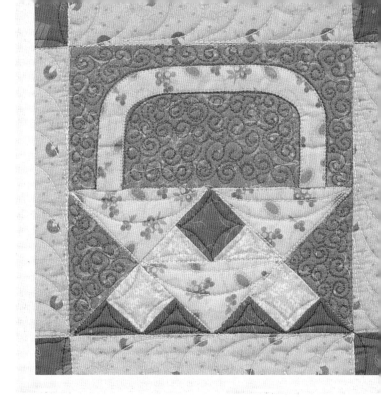

4. Join a cream or aqua B triangle and a unit from step 3 along their long edges. Make one unit measuring 2⅝" square, including seam allowances.

Make 1 unit,
2⅝" × 2⅝".

5. Sew the remaining units from step 3 to adjacent sides of the unit from step 4. Make one unit.

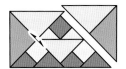 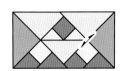

Make 1 unit.

6. Sew the long side of a unit from step 2 to the unit from step 5, making sure the lighter triangle is along the top edge. Sew the remaining unit from step 2 to the opposite side of the unit to make a basket unit measuring 3½" × 6½", including seam allowances.

Make 1 unit,
3½" × 6½".

7. Join the handle unit to the basket unit to make a Basket block. Repeat the steps to make a total of 12 blocks measuring 6½" square, including seam allowances.

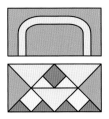 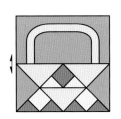

Make 12 blocks,
6½" × 6½".

WESTWARD HO

Ornate or simple, a sewing box or basket was a necessity for any pioneer family, and was one of the items frequently listed in the inventory of a migrating household. Girls learned to sew at an early age, with many charming examples of their first quilts, such as doll quilts, surviving to this day.

Making the Pieced Border

1. Draw a diagonal line from corner to corner on the wrong side of each teal 2⅜" square and cream print #2 square. Align two teal squares on opposite corners of a 4¼" red print #1 square, right sides together. The marked squares should overlap in the center. Sew ¼" from both sides of the drawn lines. Cut on the drawn lines to make two units.

2. Place a marked teal square on the red corner of a unit from step 1, right sides together and noting the direction of the marked line. Sew ¼" from both sides of the drawn line. Cut the unit apart on the drawn line. Repeat with the remaining marked square and unit from step 1 to yield four flying-geese units. Make a total of 40 flying-geese units measuring 2" × 3½", including seam allowances.

Make 40 units,
2" × 3½".

3. Place a marked cream square on one end of the unit from step 2, noting the direction of the marked line. Sew on the marked line. Trim the excess corner fabric ¼" from the stitched line. Place a marked cream square on the opposite end of the unit. Sew and trim as before

to make a border unit. Make 40 units measuring 2" × 3½", including seam allowances.

Make 40 units,
2" × 3½".

Tips for Precise Piecing

I use size 17 bridal and lace pins to pin my pieces together when machine piecing. The thin 1¹⁄₁₆"-long shaft of the pins minimizes distortion of the pieces or units I'm sewing and the small head of the pin minimizes the "lift" of the pieces from the needle plate, further lessening distortion. Because the small pin heads can be difficult to remove with my fingers, I use a sharp pair of tweezers to remove the pins, and the tweezers also do double duty by guiding the pieces that are being sewn.

I have also found that increasing the pressure on the presser foot keeps the pieces from slipping and sliding in different directions when joining small pieces, such as sewing two 1" squares together. However, for bias edges of any size, I decrease the presser-foot pressure to minimize stretching.

4. Join 11 border units to make a side border measuring 2" × 33½", including seam allowances. Make two borders. Join nine border units and two 2" red print #2 squares to make a top border measuring 2" × 30½". Repeat to make the bottom border.

Make 2 side borders,
2" × 33½".

Make 2 top/bottom borders,
2" × 30½".

Assembling the Quilt Top

1. Join four 1¾" red print #2 squares and three cream print #1 rectangles to make a sashing row. Make five rows measuring 1¾" × 23½", including seam allowances.

Make 5 rows,
1¾" × 23½".

2. Join four cream print #1 rectangles and three Basket blocks to make a block row. Make four rows measuring 6½" × 23½", including seam allowances.

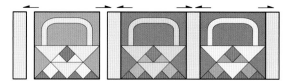

Make 4 rows,
6½" × 23½".

3. Lay out the sashing rows and block rows, alternating them as shown in the quilt assembly diagram below. Join the rows to make the quilt-top center, which should measure 23½" × 30¾", including seam allowances.

4. Sew the aqua 2½" × 30¾" strips to opposite sides of the quilt-top center. Sew the aqua 1⅞" × 27½" strips to the top and bottom edges. The quilt top should measure 27½" × 33½", including seam allowances.

5. Sew the pieced borders to opposite sides of the quilt top first and then to the top and bottom edges. The completed quilt top should measure 30½" × 36½".

Finishing the Quilt

For detailed instructions about any of the finishing steps, go to ShopMartingale.com/HowtoQuilt for free, downloadable information.

1. Layer the backing, batting, and quilt top. Baste the layers together.

2. Quilt by hand or machine. The quilt shown is machine quilted with curved lines in the basket base and loops in the block background. Feathers are quilted in the sashing and curved lines in the sashing squares. Continuous swirls are quilted in the inner border. Curved and straight lines are stitched throughout the pieced border.

3. Use the 2"-wide red print #1 strips to make binding, and then attach the binding to the quilt.

Quilt assembly

Sugarloaf

Having a proper kitchen was a joy after our frame house was completed. Sugar was in short supply at first, but after it became more readily available to us, we canned preserves and baked—pies and even cakes on occasion.

FINISHED QUILT: 20⅜" × 26⅜"

Materials

Yardage is based on 42"-wide fabric. Fat eighths are 9" × 21".

1 fat eighth *total* of assorted pink prints for Sugarloaf triangles

1 yard *total* of assorted cream, beige, brown, pink, and cheddar (orange) prints for Sugarloaf triangles

¾ yard *total* of assorted light prints for setting triangles

½ yard of cheddar orange print for border and binding

¾ yard of fabric for backing

25" × 30" piece of batting

Template plastic

4" × 12" ruler with a 45° line

Cutting

Cut all pieces across the width of the fabric unless otherwise noted. All measurements include ¼" seam allowances. Before you begin cutting, trace pattern E on pattern sheet 1 onto template plastic and cut it out. Use the template to draw a triangle onto the wrong side of the light fabrics, and then cut out the E triangles. Use a pencil and ruler to mark the ¼" seam allowance on each side of the E triangles.

From the assorted pink prints, cut a *total* of:

13 rectangles, 1⅜" × 5¾" (A)

From the assorted cream, beige, brown, pink, and cheddar orange prints, cut a *total* of:

13 sets of 2 matching rectangles, 1⅜" × 5¾" (B)

13 sets of 3 matching rectangles, 1⅜" × 5¾" (C)

13 sets of 4 matching rectangles, 1⅜" × 5¾" (D)

From the assorted light prints, cut a *total* of:

25 of piece E

From the cheddar print for border and binding, cut:

7 strips, 2" × 42"; crosscut *4 of the strips* into:
    2 strips, 2" × 23⅜"
    2 strips, 2" × 20⅜"

Making the Sugarloaf Triangles

The Sugarloaf triangles are made of patchwork diamonds, but they start with simple strip piecing. Each strip set is enough to make two pieced segments for the triangles. For each pair of finished triangles, you'll need one A rectangle, one set of two matching B rectangles, one set of three matching C rectangles, and one set of four matching D rectangles. Press seam allowances in the directions indicated by the arrows.

1. Join one each of rectangles A–D in alphabetical order, placing the A rectangle at the top and staggering the ends by 1".

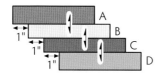

Make 1 strip set.

2. Using a rotary cutter and a ruler with a 45° line, align the 45° line on the ruler with a seamline on the strip set. Trim off the irregular end of the strip set.

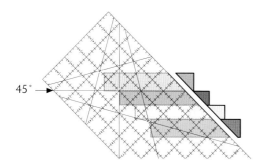

3. Rotate the strip set 180°. Measure 1⅜" from the newly cut end of the strip set and cut a 1⅜"-wide segment. Repeat to cut a second segment from the strip set.

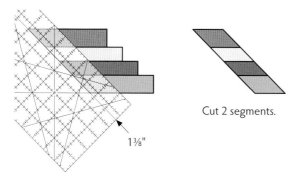

Cut 2 segments.

4. Join one each of rectangles B–D in alphabetical order, placing the B rectangle at the top and staggering the ends by 1". Trim the strip set as described in step 2. Repeat step 3 to cut two 1⅜"-wide segments.

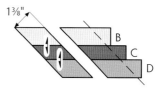

Cut 2 segments.

5. Join one C and one D rectangle, placing the C rectangle at the top and staggering the ends by 1" each. Trim the strip set as described in step 2. Repeat step 3 to cut two 1⅜"-wide segments.

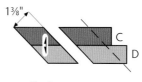

Cut 2 segments.

6. Using a rotary cutter and a ruler with a 45° line, align the 45° line on the ruler with a long edge of a D rectangle. Trim off the end of the rectangle. Rotate the rectangle 180°. Measure 1⅜" from the newly cut end and cut a 1⅜"-wide diamond. Repeat to cut a second diamond.

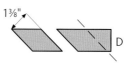

Cut 2 segments.

7. Use a pencil and ruler to mark a ¼" seam allowance on the wrong side of each segment and diamond. This step is optional, but marking the seam line and then using the Pinning Tip (see page 72) will help you achieve perfect seam intersections.

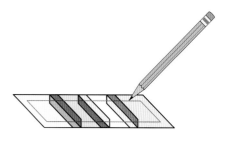

To accurately join the segments, place two segments right sides together, and insert a positioning pin through the pencil mark at the seamline on the top segment and through the pencil mark at the seamline on the bottom segment. Keep the pin perpendicular, and pull the pin tight to fully match the two segments, with the head of the pin on one side and the sharp end of the pin left free on the other side. Pin the segments together on both sides of the matched seamline and remove the placement pin. Repeat for each seam along the segment.

8. Lay out one segment each from steps 3–5 and one diamond from step 6, noting the orientation of each piece. Use a pin to match seam intersections along the marked lines. The ends of the patches will be offset by ¼". Sew the segments together along the marked line to make a pieced triangle.

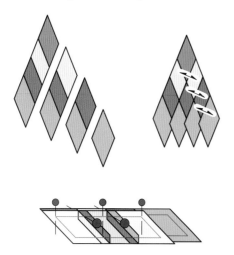

9. Trim the D diamonds, leaving a ¼" seam allowance beyond the last seam intersection. Make one more matching Sugarloaf triangle with the remaining segments from step 8.

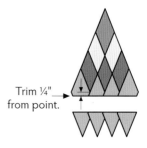

Trim ¼" from point.

10. Repeat steps 1–9 to make a total of 25 blocks. You will have one set of segments left over.

Make 25 blocks.

Pieced by Martha Walker;
quilted by B'nae Pulve

Assembling the Quilt Top

1. Lay out the 25 Sugarloaf blocks and the E triangles in five rows as shown. Sew the triangles into rows. Join the rows to complete the quilt-top center.

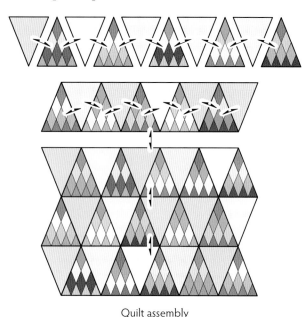

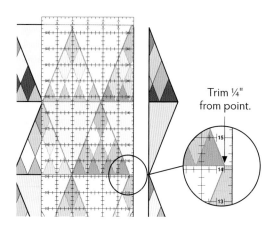

Quilt assembly

2. Using a rotary cutter and a ruler, trim and square up the quilt-top center, making sure to leave ¼" beyond the points of the crossed seams. The quilt top should measure 17⅜" × 23", including seam allowances.

Trim ¼" from point.

3. Sew the cheddar 2" × 23" strips to opposite sides of the quilt top. Sew the cheddar 2" × 20⅜" strips to the top and bottom edges. Press all seam allowances toward the border. The completed quilt top should measure 20⅜" × 26".

Finishing the Quilt

For detailed instructions about any of the finishing steps, go to ShopMartingale.com/HowtoQuilt for free, downloadable information.

1. Layer the backing, batting, and quilt top. Baste the layers together.

2. Quilt by hand or machine. The quilt shown is machine quilted with curved lines in the Sugarloaf triangles with a feather motif and a line of circles in the light triangles. Evenly spaced straight lines are quilted in the border.

3. Use the cheddar 2" × 42" strips to make binding, and then attach the binding to the quilt.

WESTWARD HO

A sugarloaf was the usual form in which refined sugar was produced and sold until the late nineteenth century, when granulated and cube sugars were introduced.

A tall cone with a rounded top was the end product of a process in which dark molasses was refined into white sugar. Pieces of the cone would be broken off with special iron sugar-cutters (sugar nips), which were shaped something like large heavy pliers. Sugar was consumed sparingly and with great care, and one loaf lasted a long time.

Farmhouse Table Runner

We discovered that the little woodlands lining Pipe Creek housed a variety of edible fruits and nuts. We found gooseberries, wild grapes, wild plum, mulberry trees, and black walnut trees growing here and there alongside the creek. In July, after we had a proper house, I ventured down to the creek and gathered buckets full of wild gooseberries, wearing thick gloves to protect my hands from the prickly stems. Later, with Mother's help, I made my first gooseberry pie.

FINISHED TABLE RUNNER: 14½" × 34½"
FINISHED BLOCK: 10" × 10"

Materials

Yardage is based on 42"-wide fabric. Fat quarters are 18"× 21".

¼ yard *total* of assorted red prints for blocks and borders

¼ yard *total* of assorted gold prints for blocks and borders

1 fat quarter of beige print for blocks

1 yard of brown print for blocks, borders, and binding

1 fat quarter of tan print for blocks and borders

⅝ yard of fabric for backing

19" × 39" rectangle of batting

Cutting

Cut all pieces across the width of the fabric unless otherwise noted.

From the assorted red prints, cut a *total* of:
62 squares, 1½" × 1½"

From the assorted gold prints, cut a *total* of:
74 squares, 1½" × 1½"

From the beige print, cut:
3 squares, 5¼" × 5¼"

From the *lengthwise grain* of the brown print, cut:
2 strips, 1½" × 32½"
4 strips, 2" × 30"
7 strips, 1½" × 30"; crosscut into:
    2 strips, 1½" × 12½"
    2 rectangles, 1½" × 10½"
    8 rectangles, 1½" × 8½"
12 squares, 2⅞" × 2⅞"

From the tan print, cut:
2 strips, 2½" × 21"; crosscut into 12 squares, 2½" × 2½"
2 strips, 1½" × 21"; crosscut into 24 squares, 1½" × 1½"

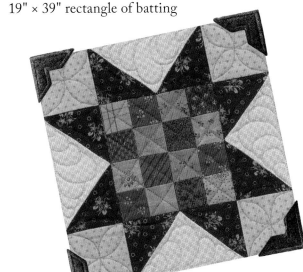

75

Making the Star Blocks

Press seam allowances in the directions indicated by the arrows.

1. Lay out two red and two gold 1½" squares in two rows of two. Sew the squares into rows. Join the rows to make a four-patch unit. Make 12 four-patch units measuring 2½" × 2½", including seam allowances.

Make 12 units,
2½" × 2½".

2. Lay out four of the four-patch units in two rows of two. Sew the units into rows. Join the rows to make a sixteen-patch unit. Make three units measuring 4½" square, including seam allowances.

Make 3 units,
4½" × 4½".

3. Draw a diagonal line from corner to corner on the wrong side of each brown square. Align two brown squares on opposite corners of a beige square, right sides together. The marked squares should overlap in the center. Sew ¼" from both sides of the drawn lines. Cut on the drawn lines to make two units.

4. Place a marked brown square on the beige corner of a unit from step 3, right sides together and noting the direction of the marked line. Sew ¼" from both sides of the drawn line. Cut the unit apart on the drawn line. Repeat with the remaining marked square and unit from step 3 to yield four flying-geese units. Make a total of 12 flying-geese units measuring 2½" × 4½", including seam allowances.

Make 12 units,
2½" × 4½".

5. Lay out four tan 2½" squares, four flying-geese units, and one sixteen-patch unit in three rows of three, noting the orientation of the flying-geese units. Sew the pieces into rows. Join the rows to make a Star block. Make three blocks measuring 8½" square, including seam allowances.

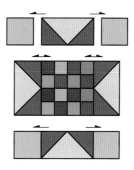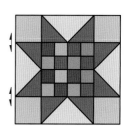

Make 3 blocks,
8½" × 8½".

Framing the Star Blocks

1. Sew brown 1½" × 8½" rectangles to opposite sides of two of the Star blocks. Sew gold 1½" squares to the ends of a brown 1½" × 8½"

**Pieced and quilted by
Martha Walker**

3. Join four two-patch units to make a strip unit. Make two units measuring 1½" × 8½", including seam allowances.

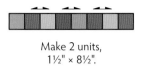

Make 2 units,
1½" × 8½".

4. Sew the units from step 3 to opposite sides of the remaining Star block. Sew brown 1½" × 10½" rectangles to the top and bottom edges to make a B block measuring 10½" square, including seam allowances.

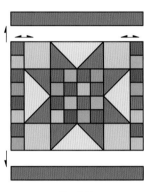

Block B.
Make 1 block, 10½" × 10½".

Making the Pieced Border

1. Sew a red square to the left edge of a gold square. Sew a tan 1½" square to the right edge of the gold square to make a three-patch unit. Make 24 units measuring 1½" × 3½", including seam allowances.

Make 24 units,
1½" × 3½".

2. Sew red squares to opposite sides of a gold square. Make two units measuring 1½" × 3½", including seam allowances.

Make 2 units,
1½" × 3½".

rectangle. Make two and sew them to the top and bottom edges of the block. Make two A blocks measuring 10½" square, including seam allowances.

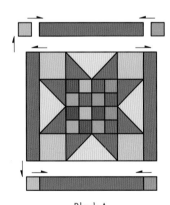

Block A.
Make 2 blocks, 10½" × 10½".

2. Sew a red square to a gold square to make a two-patch unit. Make eight units measuring 1½" × 2½", including seam allowances.

Make 8 units,
1½" × 2½".

3. Join two gold squares, nine units from step 1, and one unit from step 2 as shown to make a border measuring 1½" × 32½", including seam allowances. Repeat to make a second border.

Make 2 borders,
1½" × 32½".

4. Join three units from step 1 and a red square to make a border measuring 1½" × 10½", including seam allowances. Repeat to make a second border.

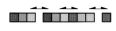

Make 2 borders,
1½" × 10½".

Assembling the Table Runner

1. Join the A and B blocks in a row as shown in the table-runner assembly diagram. The table-runner center should measure 10½" × 30½", including seam allowances.

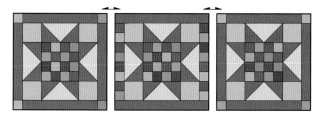

Table-runner assembly

2. Sew the shorter pieced borders to the short ends of the table runner. Sew the longer pieced borders to the two long edges of the table runner. Press all seam allowances open. The table runner should measure 12½" × 32½", including seam allowances.

3. Sew the brown 1½" × 12½" strips to the short ends of the table runner. Sew gold squares to the ends of the brown 1½" × 32½" strips and sew them to the two long edges of the table runner. Press all seam allowances toward the brown strips. The completed table runner should measure 14½" × 34½".

Finishing the Table Runner

For detailed instructions about any of the finishing steps, go to ShopMartingale.com/HowtoQuilt for free, downloadable information.

1. Layer the backing, batting, and quilt top. Baste the layers together.

2. Quilt by hand or machine. The table runner shown is machine quilted with a diagonal grid in all the small squares. Feathers are stitched in the Star block triangles, and a pumpkin-seed motif is featured in the block corners. Feathers are quilted in all the brown strips.

3. Use the brown 2"-wide strips to make binding, and then attach the binding to the table runner.

WESTWARD HO

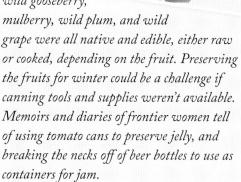

Kansas and Missouri pioneers were able to supplement their diet with a variety of fruits and nuts that were native to the states. Elderberry, pawpaw, chokecherry, wild gooseberry, mulberry, wild plum, and wild grape were all native and edible, either raw or cooked, depending on the fruit. Preserving the fruits for winter could be a challenge if canning tools and supplies weren't available. Memoirs and diaries of frontier women tell of using tomato cans to preserve jelly, and breaking the necks off of beer bottles to use as containers for jam.

About the Author

Martha Walker was 12 years old when she became mesmerized by the tiny little pieces sewn into rings in a Double Wedding Ring quilt. Made by her grandma, that quilt graced Martha's bed, and Martha became determined to make a patchwork quilt herself. At age 14 she sewed 4" squares together to make her first bed quilt. Since then, she has made many more. She is the author of four books in addition to *Prairie Patchwork*, and her designs have been widely featured in domestic and international quilting magazines.

Prior to launching her pattern company, Wagons West Designs, Martha exhibited her original designs locally and nationally. She has won numerous awards, including ribbons at International Quilt Festival, American Quilter's Society Quilt Show, National Quilter's Association Quilt Show, Pacific International Quilt Festival, Road to California, and Mid-Atlantic Quilt Festival.

Martha has channeled her love of drawing into drawing designs for cotton and wool appliqué, punchneedle embroidery, and fabric design for several fabric companies. She favors designs with a folk art and vintage appearance, with birds, flowers, berries, and holidays being some of her favorite subjects to illustrate. And when it comes to patchwork, the scrappier the better. Martha enjoys sharing her years of experience by teaching workshops on a variety of techniques and presenting trunk shows to quilt groups nationally.

Martha lives in Phoenix, Arizona, with her husband of 32 years, Thom. They have two grown sons, a daughter-in-law, and one adorable grandson.